THE
APOSTOLIC FATHERS

A New Translation and Commentary

THE APOSTOLIC FATHERS

A New Translation and Commentary

edited by Robert M. Grant,
Chairman of the Department of New Testament,
Chicago Divinity School

<table>
<tr><td>Volume 1</td><td>An Introduction
by Robert M. Grant, Chicago Divinity School</td></tr>
<tr><td>Volume 2</td><td>First and Second Clement
by Robert M. Grant, Chicago Divinity School *and* Holt H. Graham, Virginia Theological Seminary</td></tr>
<tr><td>Volume 3</td><td>The Didache and Barnabas
by Robert A. Kraft, University of Manchester</td></tr>
<tr><td>Volume 4</td><td>Ignatius of Antioch
by Robert M. Grant, Chicago Divinity School</td></tr>
<tr><td>Volume 5</td><td>Polycarp, Martyrdom of Polycarp, Fragment of Papias
by William R. Schoedel, Brown University</td></tr>
<tr><td>Volume 6</td><td>Hermas
by Graydon F. Snyder, Bethany Biblical Seminary</td></tr>
</table>

THE
APOSTOLIC FATHERS

A New Translation and Commentary

Volume 1

An Introduction

by

Robert M. Grant

THOMAS NELSON & SONS

London NEW YORK *Toronto*

DESIGN BY HAROLD LEACH

Library of Congress Catalog Card Number: 64-11546

Printed in the United States of America

PREFACE

This introduction to the Apostolic Fathers has as its function simply to introduce them. Who were they? What did they do? What did they write? What influence did they have either personally or through their writings? Such questions belong to an introduction, but the person who reads it must always keep in mind the documents being introduced. In other words, the introduction is not very useful or even intelligible unless one reads the Apostolic Fathers as well. Their statements are more important than the remarks of the introducer.

The expression "Apostolic Fathers" seems to have been used first by Severus of Antioch, Monophysite patriarch of Alexandria early in the sixth century and a great enthusiast for early Christian literature. He used the term in reference to the writings contemporary with (and therefore, by inference, those prior to) Irenaeus, at the end of the second century. The term was significant for the theological use of quotations from these writers. "Fathers" had come to mean "significant orthodox writers of the past"; "apostolic" in the early usage had referred to those who were not apostles but were disciples of apostles. The two words combined thus referred to the earliest orthodox writers outside the New Testament. In theory, it could also have been used in order to classify such New Testament writers as Mark and Luke; but they had already been regarded as "evangelists." A millennium later, the term "Apostolic Fathers" was applied to the newly discovered writings of Clement, Ignatius, Polycarp, Barnabas,

and Hermas. When those were published together by J. B.
Cotelier in 1672, he spoke of the "holy fathers who flourished
in apostolic times," and in 1699 Thomas Ittig published
Clement, Ignatius, and Polycarp in a *Bibliotheca patrum
apostolicorum greco-latina.* In 1765, A. Gallandi added the
epistle to Diognetus and the fragments of Papias and Quadratus to the traditional collection; in 1883 the discovery of the
Didache meant that one more document was available.

For our purposes, the Apostolic Fathers will consist of the
writings from the early second century or late first century
ascribed to Clement, Ignatius, Polycarp, Barnabas, and
Hermas, together with the Didache, the fragments of Papias,
and the Martyrdom of Polycarp. The letter to Diognetus
and the solitary fragment of Quadratus belong not to the
Apostolic Fathers but to the apologetic literature of the
second century and after. They were written not for those
within the Christian community but for those outside.

By excluding these documents we find that we have
pointed toward a principal characteristic of the Apostolic
Fathers. They wrote the documents we possess not for out-
siders but for those within the community of the Church.
They thus present us with "inside information" not unlike
that which we obtain for an earlier period from the letters
of the apostle Paul. No matter what the variety of literary
form may be among the writings of these Fathers, they are
all directed toward situations within the Church.

A second characteristic related to the first is that the writings are primarily practical in nature. They are not concerned
with speculative theology or, indeed, to any great extent
with theology as such. They are concerned with it only at
the point where it influences the life of Christians within the
community. Again, they are not concerned with cultural
matters. No Apostolic Father quotes Greek literature as the
apologists, or even Irenaeus, quote it; none of them betrays
more than a trace of acquaintance with Greek poetry or
philosophy. Of history they know equally little, and they

think about it even less. The only—partial—exception to these statements is provided by 1 Clement, to which we shall return later.

A third characteristic is that their thought is largely traditional. To say this is practically to reiterate what we have already said. But it is worth noting that in many respects they stand close to the New Testament writers. Polycarp stands so close that much of what he writes consists of quotations.

It should be added that this introduction is intended to introduce not only the Apostolic Fathers but also a group of commentaries on their writings. These commentaries, along with new translations, are being prepared by the editor (Ignatius) and by Professors Holt H. Graham (1 and 2 Clement), Robert A. Kraft (Didache, Barnabas), Graydon F. Snyder (Hermas), and Henry Chadwick (Polycarp, Martyrdom of Polycarp, and Papias). Naturally, the various commentators have complete freedom of interpretation (not to mention translation) and it can therefore be expected that at many points their emphasis will be rather different from those expressed in this book. No effort has been made to correlate such matters, since the editor does not believe in the existence of a single correct interpretation.

CONTENTS

CITATIONS AND ABBREVIATIONS

References to and citations from the Old Testament are usually made on the basis of the Greek version called the Septuagint (abbreviated, LXX), and for this reason the meaning as well as the chapter or verse division will often differ from the Hebrew or the English translations.

The writings of the Apostolic Fathers are given the following abbreviations:

Barn.	Epistle of Barnabas
1 Clem.	Clement of Rome to the Corinthians
2 Clem.	2 Clement (sermon)
Did.	Didache
Eph.	Ignatius to the Ephesians
Magn.	Ignatius to the Magnesians
Mand.	Hermas, Mandates
Mart. Polyc.	Martyrdom of Polycarp
Phil.	Polycarp to the Philippians
Philad.	Ignatius to the Philadelphians
Polyc.	Ignatius to Polycarp
Rom.	Ignatius to the Romans
Sim.	Hermas, Similitudes
Smyrn.	Ignatius to the Smyrnaeans
Trall.	Ignatius to the Trallians
Vis.	Hermas, Visions

In addition, the following abbreviations occur fairly often:

H. E.	Historia Ecclesiastica (Church History)
PG	J. P. Migne, Patrologia Graeca
PL	J. P. Migne, Patrologia Latina

THE
APOSTOLIC FATHERS

A New Translation and Commentary

Chapter I

THE HISTORICAL AND THEOLOGICAL SIGNIFICANCE OF THE APOSTOLIC FATHERS

One might suppose, upon encountering a good deal of the Christian theology written during the last 400 years, that after the New Testament was produced, early Christian writers became aware that nothing could be added to it— or that, if they were not aware, and continued to write, they produced literature infinitely inferior to the New Testament. To a considerable degree such a notion is due to the influence of the Protestant Reformers, who could see that there was a considerable gap between the New Testament and the writings of the Fathers of the fourth and fifth centuries. What could have happened in the interval? To be sure, fairly early in the sixteenth century printed editions of the second- and third-century Christian writers such as Irenaeus, Tertullian, Clement of Alexandria, Origen, and Cyprian became available; but the doctrine and polity reflected in their works seemed much closer to the later Catholicism than to the purer Christianity of the New Testament. Their ideas were, or seemed to be, more complicated than the simpler, more primitive faith expressed by the apostles. And when published, toward the middle of the sixteenth century, the writings of the Greek apologists of the second century suggested that after the New Testament Christianity was exposed to the pernicious influence of Greek philosophy it lost its pristine purity almost at once.

1

The problem which the Reformers faced was partly theological. Is true Christianity to be found in an ongoing, continuous tradition or in a book which provides a permanent norm? It was historical at the same time. How does one explain the difference between the Christianity of the New Testament and that reflected in the writings of the Fathers? In order to answer the second question and have some information on the basis of which to consider the first, the Reformers needed documents which, in large measure, they did not possess. These are the authentic writings of the Apostolic Fathers. But practically none of these writings was available. Latin versions of a spurious collection of Ignatius' letters and also of the Shepherd of Hermas had been published by the Catholic reformer Jacques Lefèvre d'Étaples; but 1 and 2 Clement, the genuine Ignatius, Polycarp, the Didache, and Barnabas were practically unknown. This is to say that the documents which could have made church history and the development of early Christian theology intelligible were not in existence, as far as the Reformers—and their opponents—were concerned. They could not possibly have given adequate answers to either of the two questions we have mentioned. A more satisfactory approach to early Christian history and theology became possible only in the seventeenth century, with the publication of 1 Clement, the genuine Ignatius, and the Epistle of Barnabas; the Didache was not published until 1883.

In other words, for the Reformers, early church history consisted of a series of breaks; it could be divided into periods clearly discontinuous, because the evidence which fills in the gaps was not known to them. Their periodizations, however useful to them in criticizing Greek and Roman Catholic ideas about continuity, are substantially unsound.

When we look back at the Apostolic Fathers themselves, we find them unaware of any sharp break between New Testament times and their own. And when we look at the writings which came after the Apostolic Fathers, we find a similar lack of discontinuity. The earlier Apostolic Fathers quote from the oral tradition of the sayings of Jesus just as the New Testament evangelists do; the later Christian writers such as Irenaeus, Clement of Alexandria, and Origen quote from the Apostolic Fathers and sometimes speak of their writings as scripture. We shall discuss this subject more fully in the next chapter. Here it is enough to say that at Alexandria as late as Origen's time, 1 Clement, Hermas, and Barnabas were regarded as scripture. The situation changed at the end of the third century and the beginning of the fourth, and in his festal letter of the year 367, Athanasius clearly differentiated twenty-seven New Testament books from less authoritative documents such as the Shepherd of Hermas and the Didache. The latter were useful for catechetical instruction but not for theological consideration by mature believers. The distinction meant that early Christian history was in the process of revision, although Athanasius continued to appeal to the authority of such a theologian among the Apostolic Fathers as Ignatius and, indeed, when occasion warranted, also to Hermas.

Three methods of dealing with the Apostolic Fathers gradually came into existence. (1) Their writings were regarded, as by Athanasius, as primarily useful only for catechumens, still unworthy of the mysteries of fourth-century theology. (2) Later on, theological historians of the fifth and sixth centuries created a periodization of early church history, in relation to which the Apostolic Fathers belonged to, and reflected, a period of thought in which theology was as yet not fully developed. (3) The simplest solution to the problem presented by the "bridge" of the Apostolic Fathers between the New Testament and the Platonic or Neoplatonic theology of later times was either to neglect their writings or to rewrite them in the light of later tradition. The last of these three solutions was the one most generally accepted, and the following results were obtained.

Both 1 Clement and the so-called 2 Clement, which came to be associated with it in the fourth century, were neglected; in their place, considerable attention was paid to the so-called Clementine Homilies and Recognitions, novelistic theological works which had nothing to do with the authentic memory of Clement of Rome. In addition, Clement was regarded as the author of the so-called *Apostolic Constitutions*, which were largely based upon the third-century *Didascalia Apostolorum*—which in turn used the Didache as a primary source. The genuine letters of Ignatius were interpolated in order to bring his theology up to date, and six forgeries were added to them so that his views of theology and of church polity would be in harmony with those held in the East about 360. The same treatment was applied to the Letter of Polycarp to the Philippians, and perhaps to the Martyrdom of Polycarp. Both the Didache and the Letter of Barnabas (though the latter was still included in the fourth-century Codex Sinaiticus of the Bible) were allowed to slip into desuetude. Hermas was too popular for such treatment, as papyrus fragments from Egypt prove; but his influence was felt among relatively ignorant Egyptian Christians, rather than among the learned theologians of other areas. The writings of Papias were still known to theologians—chiefly heretical—in the sixth and seventh centuries; thereafter they seem to have disappeared.

Thus, with few exceptions the church writers of the Middle Ages had a completely erroneous picture of Clement, Ignatius, and Polycarp, while they knew practically nothing of the works of Hermas, Papias, the Didachist, or the author of Barnabas.

Such a situation is not altogether surprising when one recalls the widespread influence of the writings ascribed to Dionysius the Areopagite—documents which from the sixth century onward "proved" that a convert of the apostle Paul held views completely in harmony with those of the late Neoplatonist Proclus—and also remembers that the only writing of a second-century apologist to be widely circulated was the treatise *On the Orthodox Faith,* actually written by Theodoret but ascribed to Justin.

The Apostolic Fathers had become symbols of orthodox piety, but they had done so only by losing their genuine historical characteristics and by acquiring those more congenial to theological writings of the fourth century and after.

To be sure, the authentic writings of some of them were preserved during this period. Barnabas and part of Hermas survived in the biblical Codex Sinaiticus; 1 Clement and part of 2 Clement in Codex Alexandrinus (fifth century). These manuscripts were unknown not only in the West but also in the East. The genuine Ignatius, encased in a collection of forgeries, was momentarily known to Robert Grosseteste, bishop of Lincoln in the thirteenth century, but only one Greek manuscript (now at Florence) contained them. There is a manuscript, copied in the year 1056, which includes both 1 and 2 Clement, Barnabas, the spurious Ignatius, and the Didache. But no one seems to have been aware of its existence until the late nineteenth century, when the bibliophile Philotheos Bryennios, metropolitan of Thyatira, investigated the text of Clement and the Didache.

Actually, it was not until the seventeenth century that the importance of most of the Apostolic Fathers was recognized anew. In 1623 a Calvinist theologian at Geneva published an edition of Ignatius in which he separated the genuine (though interpolated) letters of this Father, attested by Eusebius, from the pure fakes contained in all the manuscripts he knew. His work gave impetus to the work of James Ussher, Anglican archbishop of Armagh, who had come upon the Latin translation of Grosseteste in which the genuine letters were based upon a Greek original in their authentic form. Ussher produced his reconstruction of the originals in 1644; two years later the Dutch philologist Isaac Voss published the true Greek text, based on the single manuscript which he had seen at Florence.

Meanwhile Patrick Young, librarian to Charles I, had recognized the significance of 1 Clement, freshly available in the Codex Alexandrinus, which Cyril Lucar, patriarch of Constantinople, had presented to the English king in gratitude for assistance against Jesuit plots; Young's edition of 1 Clement and part of 2 Clement appeared in Oxford in 1633. In addition, a French monk named Luc d'Achery produced the first edition of Barnabas in 1645. Ussher would have anticipated him had not his edition been destroyed by a fire at Oxford.

The authentic Greek texts of Barnabas, Hermas, and the Didache were discovered in the nineteenth century. Since then, nothing significant has been added to the manuscript evidence of the Apostolic Fathers, except for the discovery of various versions of their writings in Oriental languages and, in addition, the recovery of a few papyrus fragments of the Didache, Ignatius, and Hermas.

It is most unlikely either that important fragments of these writings remain undiscovered or that early Christian writings comparable to them in value are still unfound. Whether or not future discoveries will become available, the writings of the Apostolic Fathers which we now possess provide ample material for philological, historical, and theological treatment. Given the fact of their existence, we might suppose that more adequate analysis would have been given them. The basic trouble seems to lie in the presuppositions of those who have either discussed or neglected them. On the one hand, there is a prejudice against them on the ground that they come from post-Apostolic times. If the only authentic Christianity was set forth by the Apostolic and sub-Apostolic writers whose works are contained in the New Testament, the Apostolic Fathers either add nothing to the original deposit or else reflect the decline and fall of Christianity. On the other hand, there is a prejudice against them on the ground that they are primitive. True and authentic Christianity is to be discovered by reading what the later, greater theologians wrote, either in Latin or Greek. Therefore the Apostolic Fathers represent a transitional stage which had best be forgotten. The only basis on which the Apostolic Fathers seem to be worth reading is one according to which they deserve some respect as witnesses to what the Church became as it passed beyond the New Testament period and had not yet become fully at home in the Graeco-Roman world. This is to say that the basic approach to the Apostolic Fathers must begin with a certain respect for them as historical figures, as ancestors, as links in the chain of Christian continuity—but with this respect modified by recognition of their inadequacies and limitations because of the unique historical situations in which they lived and wrote.

At first glance it may seem surprising that the writings of the Apostolic Fathers are so largely devoted to matters of church polity and discipline; these occupy most of the attention of the author of the Didache, of Clement, of Ignatius, and of Polycarp, and they are not absent from the Shepherd of Hermas. Indeed, among the Apostolic Fathers, only Barnabas, 2 Clement, and Papias have little to say about the organization of the Church. Such a primary concern is not lacking, however, in some of the principal documents of the New Testament, above all in the Pastoral Epistles but also in Paul's most practical letter, 1 Corinthians.

Historically, it is obvious that the writings of the Apostolic Fathers are different from many New Testament books. None of them, as far as we know, wrote a gospel or produced a treatise like Romans or Ephesians. But the extent of the difference can be exaggerated. The Apostolic Fathers were often concerned with practical problems to a degree greater than that reflected in the New Testament books. They were not apostles like Paul, journeying through the Graeco-Roman world in order to proclaim the gospel—though Ignatius provides a partial exception; they were entrusted with the less exciting, but sometimes more burdensome, task of ministering to congregations that the apostles had brought into

existence. Theologically, it is often claimed that their writings
are marked by a corrosive moralism which is sub-Christian
and due to the influence of their environment. This claim
is based upon a one-sided reading of the New Testament, to
which "grace alone" is regarded as the key. It also neglects
the fact that the Apostolic Fathers took for granted the reading of the Gospels and Epistles, in liturgy and otherwise.
Just as behind the New Testament lies the Church, apart
from which its books cannot be understood, so behind the
Apostolic Fathers lie not only the Church but also many of
the books which were to constitute the New Testament.
None of the Apostolic Fathers wrote, or intended to write,
a treatise on Christian theology.

The theology—or to speak more accurately, the theologies
—of the Apostolic Fathers can be inferred from their writings;
but it can be inferred only by considering the documents in
their historical contexts. These contexts consisted not only,
or even primarily, of the Graeco-Roman world and the
various forms of Judaism present in it, but, above all, of the
Christian communities in and for which they wrote, communities whose world views were shaped by scripture and
tradition and liturgy. It was in this context that the Apostolic
Fathers defended and interpreted Christian polity and discipline.

One question that naturally arises is related to the authority of the Apostolic Fathers in matters of Christian doctrine.
On the one hand, Christians who regard the Bible as the
sole authority for doctrine are not likely to regard the
Apostolic Fathers with great enthusiasm. But even on this
basis something can be said in their favor. Many early
Christian writers regarded their writings as canonical; that
is to say that they were practically on the same level as the
New Testament books; and when one remembers the vicissi-
tudes of the various New Testament books in the first four
centuries, one can readily conclude that the writings of some
of these Fathers were accepted quite as widely, and for as

long a time, as some New Testament books. There is no great gap between the Pastoral Epistles, for example, and the writings of Clement and Ignatius, or between James and Hermas. On the other hand, there are Christians who find the locus of authority not in the Bible alone but in a combination of the Bible with the Church and its traditions, including the tradition of rational interpretation. In the light of such a view the Apostolic Fathers are undoubtedly important because they reflect some of the earliest ways in which both the Bible and tradition were understood, and ways in which early Christian thinkers thought through various aspects of their religion.

Admittedly, it is possible to exaggerate the importance of the Apostolic Fathers. They may not have possessed, and they certainly do not reflect, the concern for philosophical understanding that we encounter to some extent among the apologists and, in greater measure, in the school of Alexandria and among the greater theologians of later times. They were not, and could not be, fully aware of the implications of everything they said. For this reason some of their statements, often taken out of context, were utilized by later heresiarchs or criticized by the orthodox; for this reason their writings were largely allowed to disappear in an age of Christian thought in which historical understanding was not widespread.

It is historical understanding which makes possible a realistic assessment of these Fathers' achievement. They addressed themselves primarily to the circumstances of the Church in their own time and place. To speak more accurately, we should refer to their own times and places, for these writers, like their writings, are quite heterogeneous. In the collection of writings which since the sixteenth century has been classified as "Apostolic Fathers," we find a "manual of discipline" (the Didache), two pastoral letters (1 Clement and Polycarp), a sermon (2 Clement), a lecture (Barnabas), a revelation or series of revelations (Hermas), seven semi-personal letters (Ignatius), a martyrdom (that of Polycarp), and fragments of an exegetical work (Papias). These documents probably reflect the period of time from A.D. 90 or so to A.D. 167; they come from, or are based on, the Christian life of Rome, Asia Minor, Syria, and perhaps Alexandria. Two of them present themselves, or were early presented, as the writings of apostles (Didache, Barnabas); four authors were bishops or the equivalent of bishops (Clement, Ignatius, Polycarp, Papias), while one was apparently a prophet (Hermas). The variety attested by the Apostolic Fathers is no less than the variety found in the New Testament.

This is to say that the writings of the Apostolic Fathers are almost precisely what a historian would like to have in order to be able to analyze early Christian history in the period between the New Testament and the times of the major apologists, later in the second century. They express the kind of variety which he would expect to find, as well as the underlying unity which he might hope to find. To be sure, the Gnostic thought that was being developed in this period is not conspicuously present in the Apostolic Fathers; but the notion that large numbers of early Christians were either patently or latently Gnostics is likely to be incorrect. In addition to the way in which the Apostolic Fathers fulfill historians' expectations and hopes, one should also mention the simple fact that their writings are what we actually possess. It may be more exciting to create speculations about the way in which early Christianity should have developed than to examine the way in which it actually did develop; but the genuine writings that we have should be the primary objects of the church historian's concern.

It is always possible, of course, to claim that through or underneath these writings we can envisage a situation in which they did not possess the importance we assign to them. For instance, when Ignatius vigorously defends episcopacy, he may well be facing a situation in which others did not regard it so highly. But although such a claim is undoubtedly justified, its significance must not be exaggerated. We cannot infer either that Ignatius invented the idea of episcopacy himself or that his views were shared by a minority. All we can say is that he did uphold episcopacy and that others probably opposed it in the form he advocated.

Again, to argue that, in his opposition to some form of Gnosticism, Ignatius used terms which we find among later Gnostic writings, and therefore he was strongly influenced by Gnosticism, is to misinterpret his ideas. First, a writer can share terminology with his opponents without being influenced by them; and second, it is by no means clear that in the early second century terms used by later Gnostics had a "technical sense" (or, in some instances, that they had such a sense even later). Critics who rightly argue that when Ignatius uses the phrase "the Catholic church" he does not have in mind the sense in which the phrase was later used, should not read Gnostic technicalities back from later times into his writings.

The points we have just mentioned should suffice to show that in our opinion a truly historical exegesis of the Apostolic Fathers is the only satisfactory one. But since historical exegesis conveys a variety of meanings among modern readers, we should go on to state what we mean by it. First of all, and perhaps finally, it consists of placing the writings involved in their historical context, in their setting in space and time. In the case of the Apostolic Fathers, such a placing requires us to consider what the words, phrases, and sentences they employ would have meant in the settings in and for which they wrote. Clearly we have to consider the life and thought of the Graeco-Roman world in their time, and of the kinds of Judaism which flourished in that world. But this is only one aspect of interpreting the writings in relation to their environment. The environment was certainly the Roman Empire of the late first and early second centuries; it was no less certainly the Christian Church of the same period. The Apostolic Fathers cannot be understood without keeping in mind the ongoing life of the Christian communities in and for which they wrote—the communities which read, preserved, and transmitted their writings. Conceivably the writings could have been found, as scraps of some of them have been found, in the rubbish heaps of Egypt, among the papyri. Actually the manuscripts were copied and recopied by Christians and for Christian use.

It is the importance which in various times Christians have assigned to these writings that has resulted in their preservation. They are important today because they contain the earliest reflections of Christian life outside the New Testament. They show us what, for better or for worse, the Church was coming to be. They show us the Christian life in process. Whether one views this process as a decline or a development, it did in fact take place, and Christians today, whether rejecting or accepting the ideas of the Apostolic Fathers, are their heirs.

Chapter II

THE APOSTOLIC FATHERS
IN THE CHRISTIAN CHURCH

The primary significance of the Apostolic Fathers lies in their witness to the Christian faith, not in their own personality or literary skill, important as such matters may be. It is therefore valuable to know the relationship of their writings to the Church in later times. What use was made of these Fathers themselves as symbols of the primitive faith? What use was made of their writings, and for what purposes? What effect did knowledge or ignorance of the writings have upon conceptions of the life and thought of the early Church as later writers looked back to it?

Our knowledge of the early use of the writings of the Apostolic Fathers has a definite beginning in the Letter of Polycarp to the Philippians, early in the second century, for it contains no fewer than fifteen allusions to the letters of Clement to the Corinthians, as well as many allusions to the letters of Ignatius, which Polycarp himself collected.

From the decade between 170 and 180 we possess further testimonies in regard to 1 Clement. Dionysius, bishop of Corinth, wrote a letter to Soter, bishop of Rome, in which he said that the Corinthian church had read Soter's own letter, "from the reading of which we shall always be able to obtain admonition, as also from the former epistle written to us through Clement."[1] It is possible, but not clearly stated, that 1 Clement was read in the worship of the Corinthian

[1] Eusebius, *H.E.* 4, 23, 11.

13

community; it is certain that the letter was highly valued. Further information about 1 Clement was obtained and provided by the Syrian(?) Christian Hegesippus, who visited Corinth on his way to Rome. He had learned that the letter was written during the reign of Domitian (81-96)[2] and that the Corinthian church "remained in the true faith until Primus was bishop of Corinth." Since Eusebius states that he made the latter statement "after some remarks on the epistle of Clement to the Corinthians," it would appear that he was correlating the episcopate of Primus with the letter.[3] Unfortunately we know nothing of the time when Primus was bishop.

The earliest explicit quotations from the writings of the Apostolic Fathers are to be found in the treatise against heresies which Irenaeus, bishop of Lyons in southern France, wrote about the year 185. In this treatise he clearly describes 1 Clement, and perhaps 2 Clement as well, and the letter of Polycarp.[4] In addition, he quotes from the Shepherd of Hermas and cites some words from Ignatius "as one of our people said."[5] There is a definite use of Papias, too.[6] The question of Irenaeus' use of Barnabas is unsettled, though it is clear that quotations of Isaiah 50 in both Christian writings come from the same kind of text.[7]

It is not as clear as various modern writers have assumed that Irenaeus regards any of these documents as scripture. Indeed, it may be that he knows a fairly clear line dividing what is scriptural and what is not, and that this line excludes the early Fathers.

In his time, however, or a little later, the anti-Montanist writer Apollonius seems to have viewed the Didache as

[2] *Ibid.*, 3, 16.
[3] *Ibid.*, 4, 22, 1-2.
[4] *Adv. haer.* 3, 3, 3-4; cf. B. Botte, *Revue des études augustiennes* 2 (1956), 67-71.
[5] *Adv. haer.* 4, 20, 2 (Mand. 1:1); 5, 28, 3 (Rom. 4:1).
[6] *Adv. haer.* 5, 33, 4.
[7] L.-M. Froidevaux, *Recherches de science religieuse* 44 (1956), 408-421.

scriptural,[8] and at Alexandria in Clement's time the picture was not very clear. Clement refers to both Barnabas and Clement of Rome as apostles and describes Barnabas also as "apostolic."[9] He quotes from Barnabas as from "the scripture."[10] The many quotations from 1 Clement and Hermas seem to be equally important, as does the one quotation (tacitly) from the Didache.[11] It should be noted, however, that Clement seems to have no knowledge whatever of Ignatius or Polycarp or Papias. This is to say that the writings of the Apostolic Fathers which he knows are rather Jewish in character and *may* reflect traditional usage at Rome (Clement, Hermas) and at Alexandria (Didache, Barnabas).

It may be added that where Clement is pretty clearly following some earlier Gnostic or semi-Gnostic source, there may be reflections of Ignatius. His letter to the Ephesians (18:2; 19) seems to underlie what Clement is using in *Eclogae propheticae* 7, 1 and *Excerpta ex Theodoto* 74. This is not to say that Ignatius' ideas are Gnostic; on the contrary, it is to say that the Gnostics were fascinated by certain aspects of his thought.

The real founder of the Christian school at Alexandria, Origen, has a somewhat different group of ancient writings. Origen does not know the Didache, Polycarp, or Papias, but he does provide quotations from Barnabas, Clement, Hermas, and Ignatius. The letter of Barnabas is scripture, and Origen can call it "the general epistle of Barnabas."[12] Clement, a disciple of the apostles, is mentioned in Philippians 4:3. Apparently, in Origen's view, he wrote not only 1 Clement but also the *Recognitions*.[13] In earlier writings Origen quotes

[8] Eusebius, *H.E.* 5, 18, 4 (Did. 11:12).
[9] *Strom.* 2, 31, 2; 35, 5; 4, 105, 1; 2, 116, 3.
[10] *Strom.* 6, 65, 2.
[11] *Strom.* 1, 100, 4; cf. J. E. L. Oulton, *Journal of Theological Studies* 41 (1940), 177-179.
[12] *De princ.* 3, 2, 4; *Rom. comm.* 1, 18 (PG 14, 866B), *C. Cels.* 1, 63.
[13] *De princ.* 2, 3, 6; *Sel. in Ezech.* 8, 3; *Ioh. comm.* 6, 54; *Heb. hom.* in Eusebius, *H.E.* 6, 25, 14; R. Cadiou in *Recherches de science religieuse* 20 (1930), 506-528.

Hermas as scripture; in later writings he expresses consider-able doubt about its status.[14] Finally, he knows that Ignatius was bishop of Antioch and gives quotations from two of his letters—though he certainly does not regard them as scriptural.[15]

Among other third-century writers there are few traces of the Apostolic Fathers. Tertullian knows the names of Barna-bas, Clement, and Polycarp, but he seems to make no use of their writings. His attitude toward Hermas varied. Earlier he viewed the Shepherd with some favor; later, when he became a rigorous Montanist, he thought that the Shepherd was not rigorous enough.[16] His contemporary Hippolytus of Rome may possibly allude to Hermas (Vis. 3, 4, 3) in his Commentary on Daniel (2, 13), but the allusion is extremely allusive.

At the beginning of the fourth century the traces are equally scanty. About the year 300 there is a clear reference to the Didache in Pseudo-Cyprian, Adversus aleatores 4 (Did. 14:2); there are possible allusions to Ignatius' letters in the works of two bishops of Alexandria, Peter and Alex-ander;[17] and Methodius probably, though not certainly, al-ludes to Polycarp's letter in his Symposium.[18]

Very soon afterward, however, the existence of the writ-ings of the Apostolic Fathers is fully attested in a liturgical document, the Didascalia apostolorum, and in the Church History by Eusebius of Caesarea. (1) The Didascalia is cer-tainly based on the Didache; in addition, there are traces of Clement and Ignatius in it.[19] Evidence for the use of Hermas and Barnabas is less convincing. (2) In the Church History of Eusebius the Apostolic Fathers come into the clear light

14 De princ. 1, 3, 3; 3, 2, 4; Ezech. hom. 13, 3; Matt. ser. 53; 59; Matt. comm. 14, 21.
15 Luc. hom. 6 (p. 37 Rauer); Cant. cant. prol. (p. 71 Baehrens).
16 Orat. 16; Pudic. 10.
17 Lightfoot, Ignatius II 337; PG 18, 599A-B.
18 Phil. 4:3 in Sympos. 5, 6, 8.
19 R. H. Connolly, Didascalia apostolorum (Oxford, 1929).

of day. Eusebius and his assistants made use of various church libraries in Palestine, and much of what he calls church history is really literary history. He describes the following writings.

(a) Clement, a follower of Paul and third bishop of Rome, wrote a letter in the name of the Roman Church; this letter is "acknowledged" by all. Since he uses Hebrews in it, Hebrews is not a late letter; indeed, Clement probably translated it into Greek from Hebrew. There is said to be a second letter of Clement, but no evidence attests its use by "the ancients." Dialogues of Peter and Apion, ascribed to Clement, are not genuine.[20]

(b) Ignatius, bishop of Antioch after the Apostles, wrote four letters from Smyrna (Eph., Magn., Trall., Rom.; Eusebius cites Rom. 5:1-3) and three from Troas (Philad., Smyrn., Polyc., with a citation of Smyrn. 3). Eusebius then provides a dossier of early testimonies to Ignatius, quoting Irenaeus, *Adv. haer.* 5, 28, 3 with its own quotation of Ignatius (Rom. 4:1) and adding Polycarp's two references to Ignatius (Phil. 9:1-2 and 13:1-2b).[21] (In his *Quaestiones ad Stephanum*, PG 22, 881B-C, Eusebius also provides a quotation from Eph. 19:1.)

(c) Hermas, he says, is useful for elementary instruction,[22] but it belongs among the non-canonical books along with Barnabas and the Didache.[23]

(d) Papias wrote *Expositions of the Divine Oracles* in five books and they were mentioned by Irenaeus. Eusebius does not think much of Papias, who expected the imminent end of the world, and along with the valuable traditions provided in Papias' books he mentions oddities which reduce Papias' importance. Irenaeus called Papias a hearer of John, but in Eusebius' view he was wrong; Papias belonged to the third generation of Christians.[24]

[20] *H.E.* 3, 4, 9; 3, 16; 3, 38.
[21] *H.E.* 3, 36.
[22] *H.E.* 3, 3, 6.
[23] *H.E.* 3, 25, 4.
[24] *H.E.* 3, 39.

It is clear that for Eusebius the only important Apostolic
Fathers were Clement, Ignatius, and Polycarp; the last of
these was significant also because of his martyrdom, and
Eusebius provided lengthy quotations from the early description of it.[25] Hermas, Barnabas, the Didache, and Papias
were far less meaningful to him, primarily, one would suppose, because of their emphasis upon the apocalyptic
eschatology which, in the case of Papias, he explicitly criticizes. Perhaps also, in his opinion, the three he prefers were
especially important because they were bishops and successors to the apostles. Certainly these three motifs—martyrdom,
lack of apocalyptic eschatology, and apostolic succession—
were emphasized by Eusebius as he was writing.[26]

Generally speaking, when the Apostolic Fathers were used
by fourth-century writers after Eusebius, they were used in
two ways. The more learned theologians inclined to favor
Clement and Ignatius; thus Cyril of Jerusalem cites Clement
of Rome while Basil of Caesarea certainly quotes from
Clement, possibly from Ignatius.[27] Epiphanius of Salamis
explicitly quotes from 1 Clement and, although he rejects
the Clementine *Journeys of Peter* used by the heretical
Ebionites, he makes use of the "encyclical letters" on virginity.[28]

It was among the monks of Egypt that the more "practical,"
more Jewish, among the writings of the Apostolic Fathers
were valued highly. Thus the first *Catechesis* of Pachomius,
written before 330, contains evident allusions to the
Didache,[29] and the epistle of Barnabas is echoed in Serapion
of Thmuis.[30] The fourth-century biblical manuscript, Codex
Sinaiticus, contains both Barnabas and Hermas, while there

25 *H.E.* 4, 15.
26 Cf. W. Völker in *Vigiliae Christianae* 4 (1950), 157-180.
27 PG 33, 1025B; 32, 201C; 31, 1464C.
28 *Pan.* 27, 6, 4; 30, 15, 1-2.
29 *Corpus scriptorum christianorum orientalium* 160 (Louvain, 1956) pp.
1, 6, 8-9, 13, 23, 46; cf. W. Budge, *Coptic Apocrypha* (London, 1913),
piece VI.
30 H. Windisch, *Der Barnabasbrief* (Tübingen, 1920), 302, 328.

are many papyrus fragments of the third century and later in which parts of Hermas are preserved. One papyrus fragment gives us a bit of the Didache in Greek, another, a piece in Coptic.[31]

Athanasius of Alexandria was acquainted with two writings of the Apostolic Fathers which he regarded as almost canonical. The more important of them was the Shepherd (he never names the author), which he called a "most useful book" in his early (ca. 336?) treatise *On the Incarnation;* from it he cited the beginning of the first Mandate.[32] About fifteen years later, writing *On the Decrees of the Nicene Synod,* he referred to the Shepherd's statement that double-mindedness is the offspring of the devil.[33] In the same treatise, however, he criticized the Arians for citing the first Mandate; the Shepherd is not in the canon of scripture, and the passage has nothing to do with the Son, who was not created.[34] Similarly, in his letter *Ad Afros* (369) he criticized the use of the same passage by the semi-Arian Eusebians.[35] In his *Festal Letter* of 367, he stated that "the so-called Teaching of the Apostles and the Shepherd" belong to the same class as the Wisdom of Solomon, the Wisdom of Sirach, Esther, Judith, and Tobit; the Fathers decreed that they were to be read by recent converts and catechumens.[36]

The only other Apostolic Father he knew was Ignatius, "appointed bishop in Antioch after the apostles." Opponents of the Nicene settlement had claimed that a synod at Antioch which condemned Paul of Samosata had said that the Son was not *homoousios* with the Father.[37] Athanasius quoted a letter of Dionysius of Alexandria to his namesake in Rome in order to show that *homoousios* could be used wrongly as

[31] P. Oxy. XV 1782; C. Schmidt in *Zeitschrift für die neutestamentliche Wissenschaft* 24 (1925), 81-99.
[32] PG 25, 101A.
[33] PG 25, 429C (Mand. 9:9).
[34] PG 25, 456A.
[35] PG 26, 1037B.
[36] PG 26, 1437C.
[37] PG 26, 768ff.; 776C-777A.

well as rightly, and went on to explain the decision at
Antioch in the same way. Then he quoted a sentence from
Ignatius, Ephesians 7:2: "There is one physician, fleshly and
spiritual, begotten, and unbegotten, in man God, in death
true life, both of Mary and of God." This sentence, he said,
meant that Christ was "begotten on account of the flesh (for
Christ became flesh), but unbegotten because he is not
something made and begotten but is Son from the Father."[38]

Among the Latin Fathers of the late fourth and early fifth
centuries there was little acquaintance with the Apostolic
Fathers. Augustine was directly cognizant of none of them;
Jerome knew some but not all.

Jerome certainly knew (in Greek) both 1 Clement and the
so-called epistles on virginity;[39] he was apparently acquainted
with the *Recognitions* but did not think much of them.[40]
His knowledge of Ignatius and Barnabas did not extend very
far, for of the two quotations he provides (apart from what
he takes from Eusebius), one comes through Origen and
the other is from Barnabas.[41] He may have read Barnabas
since he explains some of the Hebrew words found in the
letter.[42] He was most unenthusiastic about Hermas, to whose
Visions he referred; it was an apocryphal book full of stu-
pidity, in his opinion, and it was practically unknown among
Latin readers.[43]

A highly laudatory description of Clement by Eucherius
of Lerins in the year 432 is based on the *Recognitions,* not on
1 Clement.

In the East at this time some of the Apostolic Fathers became important because of the Christological controversies
between Alexandria and Antioch; in the course of these de-

[38] PG 26, 768ff.; 776C-777A.
[39] See P. Courcelle, *Les lettres grecques en occident* (2nd ed., Paris,
1948), 81.
[40] *Ibid.,* 82.
[41] *Ibid.,* 80.
[42] *De nominibus hebraicis* (year 388).
[43] Courcelle, *op. cit.,* 82-83.

bates, and apparently as early as the council of Ephesus in 431, the Antiochenes appealed to selected passages from the letters of Ignatius. Their favorite sections are to be found in the *Eranistes* of Theodoret, composed about 447.[44] Five came from Smyrnaeans, three from Ephesians, one from Trallians.[45]

At the same time, it was made clear by the Constantinopolitan historian Socrates that Ignatius was both devout and orthodox. The origin of the antiphonal hymns of the Church, he wrote, was in a vision in which Ignatius saw the angels singing antiphons to the holy Trinity.[46]

Under these circumstances, it was not only necessary but also rather easy for Monophysites to turn to Ignatius' writings and take out of them the passages in which his devotion led him to make somewhat unguarded Christological statements. The first witness we have to such excerpts is Timothy Aelurus, Monophysite patriarch of Alexandria, who quoted Smyrnaeans 5:3–6:1, Romans 3:3–4:1, and Romans 6:3.[47] The first was quoted from Smyrnaeans (the favorite epistle of the Antiochenes) to show that Christ's blood was from God; the second, for a clear reference to "our God Jesus Christ" now in the Father; and the third for "the passion of my God."

Non-Monophysites, naturally, preferred the texts collected by Theodoret, and it is not surprising that in the treatise of Gelasius of Rome, *De duabus naturis*, we find quotations from Ignatius, Ephesians 7:2 and 20:2, in exactly the form provided by Theodoret himself.[48]

Perhaps because of the interest in Ignatius aroused by these controversies, we find reflections of his work in two

[44] PG 83, 81B-84A; 169B; 284A.

[45] Smyrn. 1:1-2, 3:1-3, 4:2, 5:2, 7:1; Eph. 7:2, 18:2, 20:2; Trall. 9:1.

[46] Socrates, *H.E.* 6, 8 (PG 67, 689C-692A).

[47] See E. Schwartz, "Codex Vaticanus gr. 1431, eine antichalkedonische Sammlung aus der Zeit Kaiser Zenos," *Abh. Bayer. Akad.*, Philos.-philol. hist. Kl. 32, 6 (1927), 117.

[48] E. Schwartz ,"Publizistische Sammlungen zum Acacianischen Schisma," *Abh. Bayer. Akad.*, Philos.-hist. Abt. N.F. 10 (1934), 96.

papyri from Egypt, both from the fifth century. One is a liturgical papyrus in the Berlin Museum, containing an explicit allusion to Ephesians 20:2: "For a drug of immortality, an antidote of life for not entirely dying but living in thee through thy beloved Child."[49] The other is also a Berlin papyrus (P. Berol. 10581), containing Smyrnaeans 3:3–12:1.[50]

Renewed enthusiasm among the Monophysites is expressed in writings of Severus of Antioch. His homilies are full of quotations from Ignatius, and his anti-Chalcedonian treatises contain several significant passages. In his earlier work *Ad Nephalium* (about 513) he makes use of only Romans 6:3, but by the time he writes the longer *Contra impium grammiticum* (about 520), he has a longer dossier, beginning with the Romans passage but continuing with Polycarp 3:2; Ephesians 1:1; Magnesians 6:1, 8:2; Trallians 2:1, 10:1–11:1; and Smyrnaeans 1:1–2:1.[51] In addition, Severus provided quotations from Polycarp (Phil. 5:2, 12:2) and "Clement of Rome" (2 Clement 1:1).

Further proof of enthusiasm for the Apostolic Fathers in Monophysite circles is provided by an anthology written before 562 at Edessa in Syria. It begins with quotations from Ignatius (Eph. 18:1–19:1; Magn. 8:2; Rom. 6:3), Polycarp (Phil. 12:2), and "Clement of Rome" (*De virginitate* 1:5–6; 2 Clem. 1:1, 9:5).[52] Several of these quotations seem to have come from the researches of Severus, though the use of the pseudo-Clementine treatise on virginity is new.

Not everyone read the Apostolic Fathers for the purpose of theological controversy. In the White Monastery in upper Egypt, for example, monks continued to read the Didache,

49 P. Berol. 13918; H. Lietzmann, "Ein liturgischer Papyrus des Berliner Museum," *Festgabe für Adolf Jülicher* (Tübingen, 1927), 213-228.

50 C. Schmidt-W. Schubart, *Berliner Klassikertexte* VI (Berlin, 1910), 1-12.

51 *Corpus scriptorum Christianorum orientalium* Syr. IV 7, 36; IV 6, 206-207.

52 Cf. I. Rucker in *Sitzungsberichte Bayer. Akad.*, Philos.-hist. Abt., 1933, no. 5.

1 Clement, and the Clementine treatise on virginity—for edification. Papias was quoted by Philip of Side in Palestine, in his work on church history, as well as by Andrew of Caesarea in Cappadocia, in his commentary on the Apocalypse of John. The South Palestinian abbot Dorotheus (late sixth century) made use of 2 Clement 7:2 (ascribed to "the holy Clement") and probably quoted from the Didache.[53] Early in the seventh century the Palestinian monk Antiochus produced 130 "homilies" which constitute his treatise called *Pandectes*. These homilies are mosaics created almost exclusively out of older sources—including several of the Apostolic Fathers, or what Antiochus regarded as Apostolic Fathers. He makes use of twenty-three passages from six letters of Ignatius (not Romans), fifteen passages from Hermas (not the Visions), and five passages from Polycarp. In addition, there are thirty quotations from the treatise on virginity ascribed to Clement and seven from the writings being ascribed to Dionysius the Areopagite. Antiochus only once refers to the author of any of these sources, and he does so when he quotes Ignatius for the last time.[54] For our purposes his work is important because it seems to reflect the existence of a corpus of writings by early Fathers.

The corpus was, of course, continuing to undergo change and alteration. In the sixth century the picture of the Apostolic Fathers already altered earlier because of the development and circulation of the pseudo-Clementine literature, had been further modified by the introduction of a revised version of Ignatius, consisting of interpolated and forged letters, and a new Apostolic Father, Dionysius the Areopagite. The corpus of writings ascribed to Dionysius included a letter addressed to "the hierarch Polycarp" (PG 3, 1077B-1081C) and, in the treatise *On the divine names* (PG 3, 709B), a quotation from Ignatius. The pseudo-Ignatian

---

[53] Clement, PG 88, 1836B; Did. 3:1, 1661D; 3:10, 1840C; cf. H. Windisch, *Der Barnabasbrief* (Tübingen, 1920), 399.
[54] PG 89, 1821B.

letters were first used by Stephen Gobarus, who wrote about the year 575 (PG 103, 1104D).[55]

By the year 630, when the *Paschal Chronicle* was written, both Pseudo-Dionysius and Pseudo-Ignatius had become fully accepted. The former is used as a witness to the darkness at the crucifixion (PG 92, 533C), and the latter for Jesus' three-year ministry. In the chronicler's view, Ignatius was an authentic disciple of John the theologian, and had been appointed bishop of Antioch by the apostles (PG 92, 540B-C). At the end of the seventh century the *Doctrina Patrum* contains a quotation from only one Apostolic Father, and this comes from the letter to the Philippians by Pseudo-Ignatius—a letter wrongly identified as to the Tarsians.

In the eighth century the most important document for our purposes is the *Sacra* ascribed to John of Damascus, an anthology of anthologies. Its ante-Nicene sources—to which, as far as the anthologist was concerned, should be added Pseudo-Dionysius—were edited by Karl Holl in 1899.[56] They include 1 Clement (33:2-6), 2 Clement (20:1, 3, 4), and many sections of the *Homilies* and *Recognitions*. From Ignatius there are thirty-eight quotations of genuine letters (only one from Romans) and three from the interpolated, forged version (one from Trallians, two from Antiochenes). In a work certainly from John of Damascus himself (*Ep. de ieiuniis*, PG 95, 71D) there is a quotation from Pseudo-Ignatius (Philipp. 13:2-3), and we may therefore suppose that he added quotations from this version to the authentic quotations already provided in his anthology. He may simply have combined the two versions, however; his pupil Theodore of Studium used both.

More interesting than John of Damascus is Photius, who, about 855, composed a description and critique of what he

[55] On him see A. Harnack in *Harvard Theological Review* 16 (1923), 205-234; G. Bardy in *Revue des études byzantines* 5 (1947), 5-30.
[56] *Texte und Untersuchungen* 20, 2.

had been reading. Photius was not acquainted with the more definitely Jewish-Christian of the Apostolic Fathers; thus he did not know the Didache, Barnabas, Hermas, or Papias. In addition, though he knew something about Ignatius from his reading, he had not actually read Ignatius' letters. His sole direct contact with the Apostolic Fathers was provided by a little book which contained 1 and 2 Clement and Polycarp (PG 103, 405D-408B). His notes give literary and theological criticism of these works. 1 Clement was written for a situation of revolt and troubles, advocating peace and harmony; its style is clear and what one would expect from a church writer, though there are some difficulties in its content. It mentions "worlds beyond the Ocean" (20:8) and the phoenix (ch. 25), and calls Christ only "high priest and guardian" (36:1). The second epistle is primarily moral; at the beginning it calls Christ God. But like 1 Clement, it contains some expressions foreign to the divine scriptures and some strange exegesis. In both letters there is a certain lack of continuity. Polycarp's letter, on the other hand, contains sound church instruction.

It is obvious that Photius had no idea of the historical circumstances of these writings. He lived in the timeless Byzantine world and criticized early theology as if it were late. For him Clement was the author of the *Apostolic Constitutions* as well as of the shorter letters.

It was not until the eleventh century that genuine concern for early Christian writings revived, in part because of the controversies between East and West. The most important witness to this revival that we possess is a Greek manuscript, now at Jerusalem (Taph. 54), written in the year 1056. It begins with a synopsis of the Old Testament and then presents a collection of Apostolic Fathers consisting of Barnabas, 1 and 2 Clement, the Didache, and the longer version of Ignatius. Such manuscripts were to be found even in the West, where the Apostolic Fathers had been nearly forgotten.

At Namur there is a Latin manuscript of the eleventh to twelfth century which contains, among some other works, an old translation of 1 Clement.[57]

At Cambridge there is a fifteenth-century manuscript which contains a Latin translation of the letters of Ignatius, including the authentic seven in their original form. This translation, important for later studies, apparently goes back to the thirteenth century. We should say something about the translator because of his influence on the diffusion of patristic study.

One of the most important medieval students of early patristic literature was Robert Grosseteste, first chancellor of the University of Oxford (for some time from 1214) and bishop of Lincoln (1235-1253). We are fortunate enough to possess excellent modern studies of his writings, of his work as scholar and biblical exegete, and of his library.[58] In relation to the early Fathers, Grosseteste was best known as a translator. "There can be little doubt that he contributed more than any other person to the introduction of Greek learning into thirteenth-century England."[59] He brought Greek grammars, dictionaries, and manuscripts to England, and invited Greek scholars as well. Early in his episcopate he acquired several Greek manuscripts of the treatise *De fide orthodoxa* by John of Damascus and made a translation of his own by correcting the version of Burgundio of Pisa (ca. 1148-1150).[60] Not long afterward, he made a translation of the apocryphal correspondence of Ignatius with the apostle John and the Virgin Mary—according to a thirteenth-century manuscript at Tours (Bibl. munic. 247, f. 483) which reads "*epistolae transtulit de greco in latinum Magister Robertus*

[57] On this see R. Knopf, "Der erste Klemensbrief," *Texte und Untersuchungen* 20, 1 (Leipzig, 1901), 9.
[58] S. H. Thomson, *The Writings of Robert Grosseteste* (Cambridge, 1940); D. A. Callus, ed., *Robert Grosseteste Scholar and Bishop* (Oxford, 1955).
[59] Callus, *ibid.*, 36-37.
[60] *Ibid.*, 46-53.

Grossa testa Lincolniensis episcopus." But Grosseteste was probably not content to translate only these letters. He seems to have acquired from south Italy or Greece a manuscript which combined the seven genuine letters of Ignatius with the six forged epistles, and to have translated them into Latin. In the seventeenth century there were two copies of his version in existence; one survives as MS. 395 in Gonville and Caius College, Cambridge; the other, now lost, was collated by Archbishop Ussher in a copy of the Cambridge manuscript (Trinity College, Dublin, MS. D. 3. 11). It was Ussher's hypothesis that the version was made by Grosseteste, and—in spite of Thomson's criticisms[61]—it still seems convincing; the same Latin version of Ignatius is used in Grosseteste's *Commentary on the Ecclesiastical Hierarchy,* written between 1239 and 1243, and the Oxford masters of the fourteenth century provide the only other quotations from it.[62] Bishop Lightfoot added another, quite reasonable, hypothesis: that Grosseteste translated Ignatius because the letters were to be found in his manuscript of the works of Pseudo-Dionysius—as, in fact, they are found in several extant manuscripts.[63] Unfortunately for this hypothesis, R. Barbour has traced the manuscript Grosseteste used, and neither it (Bodl. MS. Canon. Gr. 97) nor the manuscripts with which Grosseteste and his assistants collated it contained the letters of Ignatius.[64]

We do not know how Grosseteste became acquainted with Ignatius' letters. Conceivably his attention was drawn to them by John of Basingstoke, archdeacon of Leicester, who visited Athens and returned with Greek manuscripts, drawing the bishop's attention to the Testaments of the Twelve

[61] Thomson, *op. cit.,* 58-62.
[62] Callus, *op. cit.,* 54.
[63] Lightfoot, *Ignatius* I 77.
[64] "A Manuscript of Pseudo-Dionysius the Areopagite Copied for Robert Grosseteste," *Actes du X⁰ congrès international d'études byzantines* 1955 (Istanbul, 1957), 115.

Patriarchs. Messengers sent to Athens brought back a tenth-century manuscript (Cambridge University MS. Ff. i. 24) of the Testaments in 1242, and with his assistant Nicholas the Greek, canon of Lincoln, the bishop translated the Testaments into Latin, in the belief that they originally formed part of the Hebrew Bible.[65]

It is a fact that Grosseteste translated Pseudo-Dionysius and the Testaments, and a probability that he performed the same function for Ignatius. The existence of his work in the thirteenth century gives no evidence of a patristic revival, but it shows how much one influential person can accomplish.

It was not until the end of the fifteenth century that the writings of any of the Apostolic Fathers appeared in printed form; and then they appeared only in Latin versions. The first editor to deal with them was the French Catholic reformer Jacques Lefèvre d'Étaples; he published in Latin the writings of Dionysius the Areopagite, the longer version of eleven Ignatian letters, and the letter of Polycarp (Paris, 1498; reprinted at Venice, 1502; second edition at Paris, H. Stephanus, 1515). Lefèvre d'Étaples was also responsible for the first printing of a Latin Hermas; this he published in his *Liber trium virorum et trium spiritualium virginum* (Paris, 1513).

Greek texts of the Apostolic Fathers were very slow to appear, apart from the writings of Dionysius the Areopagite (anonymous, Florence, 1516). It was not until 1557 that at Dillingen, Valentinus Hartung (also known as Frid or Pacaeus) published a Greek text of the interpolated Ignatius. In 1623 a much more influential edition was produced by the Calvinist professor and pastor Nicolaus Vedelius, who separated the genuine (though interpolated) letters mentioned by Eusebius from those which were simply forgeries. This edition, brought to the attention of the Anglican Archbishop

[65] Callus, *op. cit.*, 40, 55-56, 61-62 (on the manuscripts, cf. Thomson, *op. cit.*, 42-44).

Ussher early in the same year, undoubtedly encouraged the research which finally settled the Ignatian question.[66]

Before Ussher got very far, however, Cyril Lucar, patriarch of Constantinople, presented the English king with the Codex Alexandrinus of the Bible, a fifth-century Greek manuscript which included 1 Clement and part of 2 Clement. The codex reached England in 1628; five years later, Patrick Young, the librarian of Charles I, published 1 and 2 Clement.

This new edition revolutionized the study of early Christian literature. Earlier Clement had been regarded as the author of the *Apostolic Constitutions,* and we can clearly see the state of scholarship in the introduction which Franciscus Turrianus provided for his *editio princeps* of them (Venice, 1563). He stated that they were clearly authentic because they were mentioned by Athanasius (actually Athanasius was referring to the Didache) and were used in the scholia on Dionysius the Areopagite which Dionysius of Alexandria (third century) composed. (Actually the scholia were written by Maximus Confessor in the seventh century.) In Turrianus' view, Tertullian borrowed the story of the phoenix from the *Constitutions;* here, though he could not have known it, he was on firmer ground, for Tertullian may well have derived the phoenix story from 1 Clement. And finally, Turrianus held that the *Constitutions* were genuine because the ideas of Ignatius were close to them. Unfortunately, he was using the pseudo-Ignatian letters to prove his point.

Now that 1 Clement was at last available again, there was firm ground on which the history of early Christian literature, beginning with the Apostolic Fathers, could be built.

Meanwhile Ussher was continuing his work on the letters of Ignatius, aided by a Latin version at Caius College, Cambridge, of which he had learned as early as 1629.[67] In 1637 he described his progress thus:

[66] See C. E. Elrington, *The Whole Works of the Most Rev. James Ussher,* D.D., XV, 207 (letter LXV).

[67] *Ibid.,* 482 (letter CLXIII).

The MS. Latin copy of Ignatius in Caius Coll. library hath this singular in it, that in the genuine epistles (for others I heed not) those passages are wanting, which are excepted against as institutious and suppositious by our writers; and that the place touching the eucharist cited by Theodoret out of the epistle to the Smyrnians, which is wanting in all the other books, is to be found in this. But I intend ere long to publish Ignatius myself, as considering it a matter of very great consequence to have a writer of his standing freed (as much as may be) from those interpolations of later times.[68]

Arriving in Oxford in 1640, Ussher found that his correspondence suffered because "the printer followeth me here so hard, in my publishing the Epistles and Martyrdoms of Polycarpus and Ignatius"[69]—but it was not until 1642 that a date could be printed on his "old Latin version" (based on copies of the version by Robert Grosseteste), and another year elapsed before the whole edition of Ignatius and Polycarp was ready.

Meanwhile a Continental friend had brought fresh materials. The famous Dutch philologist Gerhard Voss—honorary prebend of Canterbury since 1629—had sent his son Isaac to England with a letter to Ussher and, more important, with copies of a Latin version and an incomplete Greek text of Barnabas. Impressed with the antiquity of the document, Ussher had decided to incorporate it in his edition along with some notes by the younger Voss. Voss then went to Italy to look for a Greek manuscript of the authentic Ignatius.

In 1643 Ussher's edition was finally printed. It bore the title *Ignatii, Polycarpi, et Barnabae, Epistolae atque Martyria.* Unfortunately, all but one of the copies of this edition were destroyed by a disastrous fire at Oxford on October 6, 1644—this one, incomplete, is preserved in the Bodleian

[68] *Ibid.*, XVI, 35 (letter CCXIII).
[69] *Ibid.*, 64 (letter CCXX).

Library.[70] Undeterred by this calamity, Ussher dropped Barnabas from his text, added 200 pages of critical observations to replace it, and published the work anew by the end of the year.

He had lost the race to present the *editio princeps* of Barnabas, toward which Dom Hugo Menard of Paris had been working since at least as early as 1638, when he received the approval of the Paris theological faculty (he had sent a copy of his manuscript to Archbishop Laud in 1639). After Menard's death, early in 1644, his colleague Luc d'Achery applied for the royal privilege to print the book; the printing was finished on November 30, though the title page bears the date 1645.

More important, however, was the fact that in 1646 Ussher's reconstruction of the Greek from the Latin Ignatius was fully confirmed; at Amsterdam Isaac Voss published the Florentine manuscript that contained the authentic text of all the Ignatian letters except Romans, and also provided a new edition of Barnabas, based on three manuscripts to Menard-d'Achery's one. Voss argued that the letter of Barnabas was authentic because of its parallels to 1 Clement. As he mentioned the letter of Clement, he added a warm note of appreciation to Patrick Young. It is not altogether surprising that after the Restoration he died in England as a canon of Windsor.

To be sure, some of the more conservative theologians continued to use nonauthentic documents while, on the other hand, the more radical Protestant critics, especially in France, denied the authenticity of the new documents. By the end of the seventeenth century, however, historical scholarship, largely Anglican in inspiration, had established a relatively conservative picture of the Apostolic Fathers which has been able to maintain itself fairly firmly up to the present time.

[70] The edition of Barnabas by John Fell (Oxford, 1685) was in part based upon this copy.

Attacks upon the reliability and authenticity of Clement, Ignatius, and Polycarp were met by massive counterthrusts,
notably by John Pearson, bishop of Chester, in his *Vindiciae
Ignatianae* (1672) and by J. B. Lightfoot, bishop of Durham,
in his five volumes on *The Apostolic Fathers* (1885–1890).

The rise of historical scholarship on the Continent did not
affect the study of the Apostolic Fathers as much as did the
publication of Greek texts of Hermas (1856), Barnabas (copied from the fourth-century Codex Sinaiticus by C. Tischen-
dorf in 1859), 1 and 2 Clement complete (1875), and the
Didache (1883). The last two publications were due to the
efforts of Philotheos Bryennios, who discovered at Constantinople the Greek manuscript of the year 1056, to which we
have already referred.

The most difficult problem in the modern history of the
Apostolic Fathers was presented by the Didache. Bryennios
claimed that it was written between 120 and 160, since it
made use of both Barnabas and Hermas; Harnack agreed
with him. Other critics dated it in the late second century or
even in the third century, though in recent times it seems to
have returned to the first century, where Lightfoot had placed
it. Probably the most important question at issue in relation
to it has been that of the nature of the ministry. The Didachist knows of apostles, prophets, and teachers; they are about
to be supplanted by bishops and deacons (15:1-2). The
Didache thus lends support to, and in turn is supported by,
a theory of early Christian ministry which views it as a development (for good or for ill) from the simple, "charismatic," early situation to one more complex, more carefully
organized, and later.

In his *Kirchenrecht* (1892), Rudolf Sohm argued that the
birth of Catholicism—the religion of authority rather than
the religion of the Spirit—was marked by the production of
1 Clement, with its emphasis upon submission to authority

in the Church.[71] This was one line of attack. Other Lutheran scholars found the birth of Catholicism in Ignatius, and militantly attacked him for introducing to Christianity ideas derived from the mystery religions of paganism or, in more recent denunciations, Gnosticism:[72] Some interpreters went so far as to find decline and fall in all the Apostolic Fathers— decline and fall from certain New Testament doctrines regarded as normative.[73]

The answer to such criticisms can be provided along several lines. (1) The Apostolic Fathers, who possessed many of the documents now contained in the New Testament, did not intend to reproduce them, but were trying to work out the implications of the Christian tradition in new situations. (2) The New Testament itself does not contain either a single theology (whether simple or complex) or a picture of Church and ministry purely "charismatic." The Jewish background of early Christianity, as illuminated by the Dead Sea Scrolls, has provided fresh parallels to the organization of the early Church which render the simpler solutions of earlier scholars untenable.[74] (3) The Apostolic Fathers, unlike some of their later critics, were not trying to discover or invent a primitive shapeless Christianity which could be remolded in their own image. They are primary witnesses to the continuity of the Christian tradition and to the diversity present within it.

We now turn to the content of their writings and to their relationship to earlier Christian documents.

[71] See O. Knoch, "Die Ausführungen des 1. Clemensbriefes über die kirchliche Verfassung im Spiegel der neueren Deutungen seit R. Sohm und A. Harnack," *Theologische Quartalschrift* 141 (1961), 385-407.

[72] See R. M. Grant, in E. Castelli, ed., *Ermeneutica e tradizione* (Rome, 1963), 183-201.

[73] See T. F. Torrance, *The Doctrine of Grace in the Apostolic Fathers* (Edinburgh, 1948).

[74] See, for example, E. Stauffer, "Jüdisches Erbe im urchristlichen Kirchenrecht," *Theologische Literaturzeitung* 77 (1952), 201-206; B. Reicke, "The Constitution of the Primitive Church in the Light of Jewish Documents," in K. Stendahl, ed., *The Scrolls and the New Testament* (New York, 1957), 143-156.

Chapter III

THE WRITINGS OF THE APOSTOLIC FATHERS AND THEIR RELATIONSHIP TO THE BIBLE

Now that we have seen something of the ways in which the writings of the Apostolic Fathers were preserved and transmitted—lost and recovered—we shall turn to consider the contents of the genuine documents that we possess today. These documents are as follows:

I. The letters ascribed to Clement, consisting of
   A. the letter of the Roman church to the Corinthian church (1 Clement), and
   B. a sermon preached about 140, perhaps at Rome (2 Clement);

II. The letters of Ignatius of Antioch to the Ephesians, the Magnesians, the Trallians, the Romans, the Philadelphians, the Smyrnaeans, and Polycarp of Smyrna;

III. The literature from and concerning Polycarp, consisting of
   A. his letter or letters to the Philippians and
   B. the letter of the church at Smyrna to the church at Philomelium, containing the account of his martyrdom;

IV. The Didache, or Teaching of the Lord through the twelve apostles to the gentiles;

V. The Epistle of Barnabas;

VI. The Shepherd of Hermas; and

VII. The fragments of Papias of Hierapolis.

The arrangement we have followed is based on a division

35

into two groups of writings more or less closely interrelated. First, 1 and 2 Clement were transmitted together, and 1 Clement was probably known to Ignatius, certainly to Polycarp; Ignatius and Polycarp knew each other. Second, the Didache contains materials also found in Barnabas and Hermas, and together with Papias these writers and writings reflect a common Jewish Christianity more clearly than do the other Apostolic Fathers.

I.   The Letters Ascribed to Clement

A.   1 Clement

The First Letter of Clement or, more accurately, the letter of the Roman church to the Corinthian community, begins with a salutation which in form recalls the salutations employed by the apostle Paul and in wording closely resembles the salutations of 2 Peter, Jude, and the letter of Polycarp. The author briefly explains his delay in dealing with the Corinthians' problems and then contrasts their previous situation with the disorder now prevalent, making use of illustrative parallels from the Old Testament and early Christian history, as well as from general experience (chs. 1–6). Forgiveness is still possible on the ground of repentance, obedience, hospitality, humility, and kindness (chs. 7–19). Peace and harmony are characteristic of God's universe (ch. 20), and he requires Christians to express the same virtues in their lives (chs. 21–23); he will achieve his purpose in the future resurrection of the dead, already intimated in the sequence of day and night, the growth of seeds, and the bird called the phoenix, and foretold in the Old Testament (chs. 24–26). Because of this hope, Christians are bound to approach God and perform good works as the natural consequence of faith, receiving a reward through Jesus Christ, "the high priest of our offerings," and serving in the Christian army or body (chs. 27–38). Now Clement becomes more specific. The order of which he has spoken means that offerings and services should be at fixed times and fixed places, conducted by definite persons—in the Old Testament, the high priest, the other priests, the Levites, and the laymen. Clement's point is that the Old Testament priesthood was analogous to the Christian ministry, derived from God through Jesus Christ and the apostles. These apostles appointed bishops and deacons, just as Moses made decisions about the priesthood. They provided for the succession of other men to the episcopate—that is, of presbyters. The Old Testament shows that those who persecute the righteous (analogous to the presbyters) are not holy but wicked. Those at Corinth who advocate and practice schism are rending the members of Christ; they are worse than those whom the apostle Paul criticized in his letter (chs. 39–47). Clement continues with an appeal for the reconciliation and an exhortation to love; he asks forgiveness for his own sins and urges his readers to confess theirs. Moses asked forgiveness for his people; those responsible for the schism at Corinth should accept voluntary exile, just as "gentile" leaders have accepted it in the past. Humility is important; "whom the Lord loveth he chasteneth." Therefore the Corinthian schismatics must return to obedience to the presbyters, which is equivalent to obedience to the name of God. Disobedience to the words spoken by God through Clement is sin (chs. 48–59). The letter ends with a prayer in which the major themes are reiterated, with an explicit summary of the letter, with two benedictions, and with a statement about the venerable representatives of the Roman church who are to report back to Rome concerning the restoration of good order (chs. 59–65).

One of the most significant features of Clement's letter is the mixture of scriptural and nonscriptural motifs in it, as Werner Jaeger vigorously pointed out. The whole tone of the first few chapters is close to that of Greek rhetoricians defending the political structure of the city-state. The transition from ancient to modern models in chapter 5 is rhetorical, as is the generalization with which the examples come to an end: "Jealousy and strife have overthrown great cities and uprooted mighty nations." Though the description of cosmic harmony in chapter 20 has a few parallels in Jewish literature, it seems closer to Stoic analyses of the situation; and the story of the phoenix in chapter 25 is clearly Roman in origin. Clement assumes that the discipline of the Roman army is a good thing and that the church should be like the army (ch. 37). No Augustine, he regards pagan virtues as virtues, not as splendid vices (ch. 55). The rulers and governors of the state derive their power from God, to whom Clement prays that they may be given health, peace, concord, and firmness (ch. 61).

What is the date of Clement's letter to the Corinthians? Clearly it comes from a time after the apostolic age, for Clement can look back to the period of the martyrdoms under Nero not only as modern (as compared with the history of Israel) but also as past (5:1; 7:1-2). Christianity is old enough to be viewed as a tradition (7:2; cf. 51:2), and some Roman Christians have lived in the community "from youth to old age" (63:3). These points suggest that the letter was written in the reign of Domitian (A.D. 81–96).

It has often been suggested that the "sudden and repeated misfortunes and calamities" to which Clement refers at the beginning of the letter were attacks upon Christians toward the end of Domitian's reign. Unfortunately, as K. Lake has pointed out, "we know very little about the alleged persecution in the time of Domitian," and to relate one obscurity to another does not greatly advance historical understanding. Similarly, the fact that a consul named Titus Flavius Clemens was executed in 95, possibly because he was interested in Judaism, is not enough to connect our Clement with him or even with his household. What we know of our Clement must be derived from his letter.

Was he bishop of Rome? Irenaeus, nearly a century later, certainly thought so, and it is obvious that the author of the letter held an important and powerful position in the Roman church. It would seem likely that he himself was a presbyter-bishop, like those whose position at Corinth he was defend-ing. Around the same time or a little later the Roman Chris-tian Hermas was told to send a book to Clement, who would forward it to "the cities outside" (Vis. 2, 4, 3). Clement was probably among "the elders who preside over the church"; in other words, he had episcopal functions. That he was sole bishop of Rome is something we can hardly demonstrate.

It is sometimes supposed that because of his common sense Clement reflects a sharp decline from the norm of New Tes-tament faith. This kind of supposition, of course, neglects the Old Testament wisdom literature and the epistle of James; perhaps more surprisingly, it disregards the whole method of argumentation to be found in the Pauline epistles. To be sure, Paul speaks of the teaching of Nature only once (1 Cor. 11:14), but the idea is common in his letters. He does not rely solely upon revelation when he is discussing theology.

Insofar as Clement does rely upon revelation, which books does he use? (This question is not quite right, since Clement regards the phoenix as an expression of revelation [26:1].) Certainly he uses the Old Testament, "the holy scriptures, which are true and given through the Holy Spirit" (45:2). For him it evidently includes the law, the prophets, and the writings; and the writings certainly include the book of Ju-dith, probably Sirach and the Wisdom of Solomon. As for the New Testament books, Clement certainly knows 1 Corin-thians (47:1-4; etc.), Romans (35:5-6), and Hebrews (ch. 36), possibly other Pauline epistles and the book of Acts. His quotation from "the words of the Lord Jesus" is especially interesting. He refers to "doing what is written"—with a quo-tation from Jeremiah—and speaks of "especially, remembering the words of the Lord Jesus." After he quotes these he men-tions "this commandment" (presumably from Jeremiah) and "these injunctions" (presumably the words of Jesus) and then refers to "his hallowed words" (presumably those of Jesus) and "the holy word" (a quotation from Isaiah). It may be argued that his terminology is rather vague. It *is* rather vague, but it is clear enough so that we can see that the words of Jesus do not belong to what Clement classifies as scripture.

How does Clement know these words? This question has recently been discussed by Helmut Koester, who claims that Clement relies not upon written Gospels but upon oral tradition. Here we must proceed to quote the text (13:2), along with the synoptic parallels.

1 Clement	Matthew	Luke
Be merciful,	Cf. 5:7 (?)	Cf. 6:36-37
so that you may obtain mercy;		
Forgive,	Cf. 6:14-15	
so that it may be forgiven you;		
As you do,	Cf. 7:12	Cf. 6:31
so it will be done to you;		
As you give,		Cf. 6:38
so it will be given you;		
As you judge,	Cf. 7:1-2	
so you will be judged;		
As you are kind,		
so kindness will be shown you;		
By the measure you measure,	7:2	
by it it will be measured to you.		

None of these parallels is exact and we should agree with Koester that Clement did not make use of the written Gospels of Matthew and Luke; instead, he relied upon oral tradition. A similar situation obtains in 1 Clement 46:8.

1 Clement	Matthew	Luke
Woe to that man;	26:24 (Mark 14:21)	22:22
it were good for him not to be born	26:24 (Mark 14:21)	
rather than to scandalize	Cf. 18:6 (Mark 9:42)	17:1-2
one of my elect;		
it were better for a millstone		
to be put on him and		
for him to be drowned in the sea		
than to turn aside		
one of my elect.		

Again, the parallels are by no means close enough to prove that Clement was using written Gospels. He refers, as a matter of fact, to "the words of our Lord Jesus."

In four passages Clement quotes from documents which we do not know. Perhaps from an apocryphal version of Ezekiel he quotes the following (8:3): "Repent, O house of Israel, from your lawlessness; say to the sons of my people, 'If your sins reach from the earth to the heaven, and if they are redder than scarlet and blacker than sackcloth, and you turn to me with all your heart and say, Father, I will listen to you as a holy people.'" Another verse (17:6) seems to refer to Moses: "I am smoke from a pot"—but we do not know where Clement found it. Again, in chapter 23 we find a quotation also shared with 2 Clement (with some variations).

1 Clement	*2 Clement 11:2-4*
Wretched are the double-minded,	Wretched are the double-minded,
who doubt in their soul and say,	who doubt in their heart and say,
We heard those things	We heard those things long ago,
even in the time of our fathers,	even in the time of our fathers,
and behold, we have grown old	and awaiting them day by day
and none of these things has	we have seen none of them.
happened to us. O foolish men!	Foolish men!
Compare yourselves to a tree;	Compare yourselves to a tree;
take the vine; first it sheds	take the vine; first it sheds
its leaves, then there comes a	its leaves, then there comes a
bud, after this the unripe grape,	bud, after this the unripe grape,
then the full bunch.	then the full bunch.
	So also my people has had tumults
	and tribulations; later it will
	receive good things.

According to 2 Clement, the quotation comes from "the prophetic word," but we do not know the work in question. Finally, according to 46:1, "It is written, Unite with the holy, for those who unite with them will be made holy." The thought, but not the form of expression, recalls 1 Corinthians 6:16 and 7:14.[1]

For Clement, then, the primary written authority must be the Old Testament, including apocryphal writings; second to it seems to be a collection of Pauline (and other?) epistles. The authority of the words of Jesus does not come from their being written down. The authority of Clement's own words is quite high: God speaks through him (59:1) and he writes "through the Holy Spirit" (63:2).

The question of the relation of 1 Clement to the Gospel of John is not easy to answer. Two articles appeared in 1947 and 1948 that seem to have presented the most convincing parallels, most of them related to prayer and church order. Thus M. E. Boismard[2] found the following examples:

John	1 Clement
17:3 This is eternal life, for them to know thee, the only true God, and Jesus Christ whom thou hast sent.	43:6 to glorify the Name of the true and only God. . . . (cf. 59:3-4)
17:17 Consecrate them in the truth; thy word is truth.	60:2 Cleanse us with the cleansing of thy truth.

Two other parallels are mentioned by C. C. Tarelli.[3]

John	1 Clement
20:21 (cf. 17:18) As the Father sent me, so I send you.	42:1 The apostles received the gospel for us from the Lord Jesus Christ, Jesus the Christ was sent from God.
14:15 If you love me, keep my commandments.	49:1 He who has love in Christ should perform the commandments of Christ.

[1] The statement of K. Lake in regard to the book of Eldad and Modat, mentioned in Hermas, Vis. 2, 3, 4, that "it is thought to be quoted in II Clem. xi. 2" suffers from a complete lack of supporting evidence.

[2] "Clément de Rome et l'Évangile de Jean," Revue biblique 55 (1948), 376-387.

[3] "Clement of Rome and the Fourth Gospel," Journal of Theological Studies 48 (1947), 208-209.

John	1 Clement
6:51 . . . if anyone eats of this bread he will live forever; and the bread I will give is my flesh for the life of the world.	49:6 our Lord gave his blood . . . for us, and his flesh for our flesh, and his life (soul) for our lives (souls).

These passages do not seem to be closely enough related to provide proof that Clement knew the Gospel of John, though it is obvious that the ideas and expressions involved are fairly similar. This is to say that the context of 1 Clement was not absolutely different from that of John. Both reflect a kind of early Christianity influenced first by Judaism, second by Greek expressions. The passages mentioned are close to Jewish Christianity.

Clement is much concerned with Old Testament personages, chiefly because they provide examples or demonstrations of the points, largely moral, which he is making. Such examples are taken from various kinds of materials (63:1); Clement can ask his readers to consider the examples of God (33:8), of Jesus (16:17), of Peter and Paul and other martyrs (5:1–6:1), of Old Testament heroes (46:1), and of famous gentiles who sacrificed themselves.

He likes to list cases in which his themes are especially clear—for example, jealousy (chs. 4–5); repentance (chs. 7–8); obedience (chs. 9–12); humility (chs. 17–18); and so on. In referring to the heroes whom he mentions he often uses laudatory titles such as "our father" for Adam (6:3), Abraham (31:1), and Jacob (4:8); "the friend" for Abraham (10:1; 17:2); "the servant of God" (4:12; 43:1; 51:3; 53:5) or "faithful with all his house" (17:5; 43:1) for Moses; and "the blessed" of Moses (43:1), Paul (47:1), and Judith (55:4).

The references in chapter 55 are especially interesting. Clement begins by referring to examples of voluntary self-sacrifice or exile among the gentiles—though he names no names. Then he says that

we know that many among ourselves have *given themselves*
to bondage in order to ransom others; many have *given*
themselves to slavery and with the price they received have
fed others.

This strange little section seems to be based on Paul's language in 1 Corinthians 13:3 (in ch. 49 Clement has paraphrased 1 Cor. 13:4-7), and perhaps on a rather literal interpretation of 1 Corinthians 9:19 ("though free from all I
enslaved myself to all"). This is suggested by the combination
of the words in italics above; they come from the verse in
1 Corinthians. After Clement has given this statement, he
goes on to the classical theme of women who behave in manly
fashion; he illustrates it quite unclassically from Judith and
Esther.

B. 2 Clement

The so-called Second Letter of Clement is neither a letter
nor by Clement. Actually it is a sermon which deals first with
self-control (15:1) and more generally with exhorting the
hearers to repentance and thereby to salvation and life
(19:1). Gentile converts have turned to Jesus Christ as to
God, abandoning material idols or "dead gods"; they must
acknowledge him as Lord by their deeds. This kind of ac-
knowledgment involves asceticism, for "our stay in this world
of this flesh is slight and brief, but the promise of Christ is
great and marvelous, and it is rest in the coming kingdom
and in eternal life" (chs. 1-5). Serving Mammon implies
adultery, seduction, love of money, and deceit, all characteristic of this world; serving God for "that world" means fore-
going such things. Life is a contest for an imperishable prize
(chs. 6-7). Repentance means keeping the flesh pure and the
seal (of baptism) undefiled, for the flesh will be raised by
God; doubt about this results in wretchedness (chs. 8-11).
We wait for the kingdom of God which the Lord himself
said would come "when the two are one and the outside as

THE WRITINGS OF THE APOSTOLIC FATHERS

the inside and the male with the female neither male nor female"; we must repent so that the name of God will not be blasphemed (chs. 12–13). If we do God's will, we shall belong to the spiritual Church of life, prefigured in the creation story, where the male is Christ, the female is the Church. We should accept God's gift while we still have time, and, above all, should give alms—better than either prayer or fasting (chs. 14–16). The Lord will come; give heed to the exhortation and have faith (chs. 17–20).

The biblical quotations in 2 Clement present an interesting picture. There are two introductory formulas which clearly refer to books: "the scripture says" (2:4: Matt. 9:13; 6:8: Ezek. 14; 14:1: Jer. 7:11; 14:2: Gen. 1:27) and "the prophetic words says" (11:2-4; cf. 1 Clem. 23:3-4). Other formulas refer to the speakers: "God says" (13:4: Luke 6:32, 35; 15:3: Isaiah 58:9) or "the Lord said" or "the Lord says" or "he (the Lord) says" (references to Isaiah and Matthew). These formulas are virtually synonymous, for the author can say "the Lord says in the gospel" (8:5) or "he (the Lord) says in Isaiah" (3:5) or "the scripture says in Ezekiel" (6:8) without any apparent differences in meaning. In the author's view, "we must think of Jesus Christ as of God" (1:1) and there is therefore practically no difference between "the books and the apostles" (14:2).

From the Old Testament he gives quotations from Genesis and from the three major prophets; from the New Testament he gives quotations from Matthew, Mark, and Luke, and perhaps from an apocryphal gospel. In addition, there are allusions either to 1 Corinthians 2:9 or to a similar oral tradition (11:7; 14:5), and the exegesis of Genesis in 2 Clement 14 seems to reflect Ephesians 5:23-29. Helmut Koester has argued that in 2 Clement there is no trace of Mark (but the quotation in 2:4 is actually as close to Mark as to either Matthew or Luke), and that the quotations supposedly from Matthew and Luke actually come from a written collection

of the Lord's words, "like the collection from Oxyrhynchus."[4]
But this collection has now been identified as belonging to
the apocryphal Gospel of Thomas, to which the author would
probably, or indeed certainly, not refer as "scripture." It
seems more likely that he made use of various kinds of materials, no doubt including some of those which the author of
Thomas employed; for the saying ascribed to Jesus in
2 Clement 12:2 is remarkably close not only to the Gospel of
the Egyptians but, even more, to the twenty-second saying
in Thomas.

For the provenance and the date of 2 Clement little but
conjecture can be offered. It is possible that the document
was known to Justin, almost probable that it was known to
Irenaeus.[5] These possible relationships *may* suggest that its
origin is to be sought at Rome. More conclusive indications
of a Roman origin are to be found in (1) its association with
1 Clement, and (2) the resemblances between its view of the
Church with that found in Hermas.[6] In addition, its use of
the expression "Father of Truth" and its similarity to the
Gospel of the Egyptians may indicate that Gnostic terms and
traditions were not recognized as Gnostic in the place and at
the time in which the author wrote. Rendel Harris suggested
that he was the Encratite heretic Julius Cassianus,[7] but
there seems to be nothing peculiarly Encratite about the
document. If we may venture a wild hypothesis or guess, we
should suggest that the author was Hyginus, bishop of Rome
about 138 to 142, in whose time the Gnostic teacher Cerdo
was active there and two other Gnostics, Valentinus and Marcion, came to the city without being rejected by the church.
In the homily there is a firm grasp upon the essentials of the

[4] *Synoptische Überlieferungen bei den Apostolischen Vätern* (Berlin,
1957), 62-111.
[5] R. Knopf, *Die Lehre der zwölf Apostel. Die zwei Clemensbriefe* (Tübingen, 1920), 152; B. Botte in *Revue des études augustiniennes* 2 (1956),
67-71.
[6] See H. Windisch in *Harnack-Ehrung* (Leipzig, 1921), 134.
[7] *Zeitschrift für die neutestamentliche Wissenschaft* 23 (1924), 193-200.

traditional faith, as well as a certain vagueness about a few details, which seems to reflect the time, if not the person, of Hyginus.

II. The Letters of Ignatius of Antioch

The genuine letters of Ignatius were evidently collected by Polycarp, who wrote to the Philippians as follows (13:2):

We have sent you, as you asked, the letters of Ignatius, those sent us by him and the others which we had with us. They are attached to this letter, and you will be able to derive great benefit from them.

Ignatius, bishop of Antioch in Syria, had been taken under guard across Asia Minor to Smyrna and thence up to Troas, whence he sailed to Neapolis in Macedonia, on his way to martyrdom at Rome. From Smyrna he had written letters to the nearby churches of the Ephesians, the Magnesians, and the Trallians, all of which had sent representatives to greet him; he also wrote ahead to the Romans, urging them to "refresh" other martyrs from Syria but not to attempt to prevent his martyrdom. When he reached Troas he was joined by two Christians who had passed through Philadelphia on their way to be with him, and he wrote to the Philadelphians about the problems of their church, as well as to the Smyrnaeans and to Polycarp. He told Polycarp that though he had intended to write to all the churches (cf. Rom. 4:1) he could not do so because he was "suddenly sailing from Troas to Neapolis"; therefore Polycarp was to write to "the churches ahead" (8:1). Polycarp did not actually write to the Philippians until Ignatius had already passed through Philippi (just east of Neapolis); and it was at that point that he sent them the Ignatian letters to which he referred. Presumably his collection included copies of the four letters sent from Smyrna and the two which he and the Smyrnaeans had re-

ceived from Troas; he may have had the letter to the Philadelphians as well.

The date of the Ignatian letters is hard to determine. In
his *Chronicon*, written early in the fourth century, Eusebius
of Caesarea placed Ignatius' martyrdom in the year 107 or
108, but we do not know why he did so. The only date in
Ignatius' own letters is that which he gives for his letter to
the Romans—the ninth day before the kalends of September
(August 24); but no year is mentioned. Origen says that
Ignatius was second bishop of Antioch after the apostle Peter,
but this does not help much, except to suggest that he did
not live long after the beginning of the second century. The
conventional date assigned by most modern historians, in the
reign of Trajan, is rather likely to be correct; it is also rather
vague, since Trajan reigned from 98 to 117. But greater pre-
ciseness is not likely to be obtained.

Scholars have sometimes supposed that Ignatius belongs
to a later period, such as during the reign of Hadrian (117–
135), but the grounds for this theory lie chiefly in a notion
of the development of Christian faith and order for which
there is no evidence. We therefore retain the Trajanic date.

Structure

The letters begin with salutations, usually rather extensive
and often modeled upon those of the Pauline epistles, in
which Ignatius sets forth the unity of his faith with that of
his correspondents and, more often than not, refers to the
centrality of the passion of Jesus Christ. Especially in the
letter to the Romans he piles up honorific compounds of
adjectives and nouns in order to show the esteem in which
he holds the congregation. The letters to churches are addressed to entire communities—like most of the Pauline epistles—although Ignatius also directs part of another letter to
the bishop of Smyrna. In all the letters to communities whose
bishop Ignatius knows (except to Smyrna, since he is also

writing to Polycarp) he then proceeds to speak of the bishop and his personal qualities.

The main body of each letter is constructed in a way that depends on the problem of the church concerned; the problem of heresy is central in the letters to all the churches except that at Rome; to the Romans Ignatius has a personal request to make.

At the end of each letter Ignatius speaks of the circumstances of the church in Syria, asking for prayers for it in the first four letters and discussing the effect of the prayers in the last three. The letters usually terminate with personal notes.

Style

In style the letters are notable for a certain exuberance and wordiness typical of the "Asianic" rhetoric of Ignatius' day. In this kind of rhetoric one also finds a fondness for paradox and antithesis, which is in Ignatius' writing too; but Ignatius' leaning in this direction expresses not only his literary training but also his theological attitude, based in large measure on the Pauline epistles. These epistles not only gave him theological insights but also shaped his expression of them. In addition, as Perler has pointed out, he owes much to the Asianic diatribe known as 4 Maccabees.

This is not to say that Ignatius is nothing but a conglomerate of sources. His style, like his thought, is extremely individual and personal. Just as 1 Clement reflects the *gravitas* which was to mark the attitude of Roman Christianity, and obviously expresses the writer's own personal attitude as well, so Ignatius personifies the mystical piety of Eastern Orthodoxy. The vividness of his thought and language sets the tone for latter times.

One of the most obvious traits of his vocabulary is the use of polysyllabic compounds, often beginning with the prefixes *axio-* ("worthy") and *poly-* ("much" or "many") or ending with the suffix *-phoros* ("bearing" or "carrying"). He is also fond of elaborate metaphors, the most famous of which are

found in the ninth chapter of Ephesians. Ephesian Christians
did not permit evil doctrine to be "sown" among them but
"stopped their ears," since they are "stones of the temple of
the Father, prepared for the building of God the Father,
lifted to the heights by the crane of Jesus Christ (the cross)
and using the Holy Spirit as a rope." Alternatively, "faith is
your rope and love is the way which leads up to God." The
figure then changes to that of a religious procession. "You
are all fellow travelers, God-bearers and temple-bearers,
Christ-bearers, shrine-bearers, in every way adorned with the
commandments of Jesus Christ." The mixture of metaphors
clearly reflects Ignatius' impetuous, pictorial-minded imagi-
nation.

A rather striking feature of Ignatius' style and thought,
already noticed by Lightfoot but somewhat more frequently
exemplified than he supposed, is what we may call the "statement of reciprocity." This occurs no fewer than thirteen
times. Sometimes it involves an idea of past or present
reward.

It is fitting to glorify Jesus Christ/ who has glorified you
(Eph. 2:2).
You received my deacons/ as the Lord received you (?)
(Philad. 11:1).[8]
He who knows the bishop/ has been honored by God
(Smyrn. 9:1).
Be patient with one another/ as God is with you (Polyc.
6:2).

More often the reward is envisaged as future.

Crocus has refreshed me/ may the Father so refresh him
(Eph. 2:1).
Much is lacking to us/ so that we may not lack God (Trall.
5:2).
Desire my death/ so that you also may be desired (Rom.
8:1).

Appoint a deacon to glorify the Name/ so that you may be
glorified (Philad. 10:1).

You received my deacons/ as may the Lord receive you (?)
(Philad. 11:1).[8]

Burrhus was sent as a mark of honor/ the Lord will honor
them (Philad. 11:2).

You have refreshed me in every way/ may Jesus Christ refresh you (Smyrn. 9:2).

You are not ashamed of my bonds/ Jesus Christ will not be
ashamed of you (Smyrn. 10:2).

Burrhus refreshed me in every way/ grace will reward him
in every way (Smyrn. 12:1).

We must endure for the sake of God/ so that he will endure
us (Polyc. 3:1).

Pay attention to the bishop/ so that God will pay attention
to you (Polyc. 6:1).

A clue to this manner of expression may lie in Smyrnaeans
5:1, where Ignatius says that "there are some who ignorantly
deny him, or rather have been denied by him"; here his language recalls Galatians 4:9, where Paul speaks of "knowing
God, or rather having been known by God." Bauer refers to
this verse and also to 1 Corinthians 13:12 ("then I shall
know as I have been known") and 1 John 4:10-11, 19. None
of these passages is exactly like what Ignatius says, but he
may take his point of departure from them.

Circumstances

Ignatius wrote the first four letters from Smyrna, where he
had gone from Antioch, under a guard of ten Roman soldiers,
by the overland route through Philadelphia. There he was
visited by Onesimus, bishop of Ephesus, the deacon Burrhus,
and three others whose names but not functions are stated
in his letter back to Ephesus. Another visitor was Damas of
Magnesia with two presbyters and one deacon; Polybius of
Tralles also came to see him. To these churches Ignatius ad-

[8] We list this passage twice because no verb is expressed.

dressed letters concerning their special problems; he also
asked the Ephesian church for the continued services of the
deacon Burrhus and hinted that he would like those of Crocus. When he also wrote ahead to the Roman church, he
mentioned that he was writing "by the blessed Ephesians"
and mentioned Crocus, "a name very dear to me"—perhaps
because the Ephesians were permitting him to use Crocus as
a courier to Rome.

From Smyrna, Ignatius was taken to Troas, the port from
which he was to sail to Neapolis in Macedonia and continue
on his way to Rome. There he recalled the difficulties he had
encountered in Philadelphia (Philad. 6:3–8:2) and spoke of
the Cilician deacon Philo and the Syrian Rheus Agathopous,
who had now caught up with him. He was using the services
of Burrhus as a scribe. In a farewell letter to the Smyrnaeans
he mentioned Burrhus, Philo, and Rheus Agathopous again
(the last two had passed through Smyrna). Finally, he wrote
to Polycarp, asking him to inform the churches on the road to
Rome about his coming; those who could were to send messengers, while others were to send letters.

Along with his concern for the churches from Asia Minor
to Rome, Ignatius was also worried about affairs in Antioch.
First, there were Syrians who had already reached Rome "for
the glory of God," and the Romans had to be informed about
them (Rom. 10:2). More important, there was the situation
of the church in Syria. Ignatius simply asks the Ephesians,
the Magnesians, and the Trallians to pray for the church in
Syria, but in writing the Romans, he expresses a little more
of what is in his mind. Because the bishop of Syria is going
from east to west, from sunrise to sunset, the Syrian church
has no human bishop; its shepherd is God the Father and its
bishop is Jesus Christ—and the love of the Roman church.

By the time he reaches Troas, however, he has heard—
presumably from Philo and Rheus Agathopous—that the
church at Antioch is at peace; indeed, a council is assembling
there, to which the nearest churches have sent bishops, while

those farther away have sent presbyters and deacons. The church has recovered its greatness and its proper constitution has been restored. He urges the Philadelphians to send a deacon but does not specify the rank of the delegate to be sent by the Smyrnaeans and Polycarp. Presumably the conflict at Antioch concerned the person of Ignatius' successor. The conjecture that it involved the question of episcopacy as such has nothing to commend it. As he had said to the Trallians (3:1), without the threefold ministry there was no church. The church of Antioch could not function as a church without the presence of a bishop.

In all the letters to churches (except that to the Philadelphians, with which his relations are perhaps not as cordial as might be desired), Ignatius speaks of the church in Syria and then uses language from 1 Corinthians 15:8-10, which indicates that he regards his situation as like the apostle's. He is the least of the Syrian Christians; he is not worthy to be called one of them; he is an "abortion"; but he has obtained mercy by God's grace. Perhaps the clue to this language lies in the idea that only through martyrdom can he reach God. Since this is his view, the fact that other prospective martyrs have preceded him to Rome from Syria would encourage a feeling of unworthiness in comparison with them. "Tell them that I am close at hand" (Rom. 10:2). Ignatius feels unworthy to be called a Christian because others in his community went to martyrdom before him, just as Paul felt unworthy to be called an apostle because he had persecuted the Church of God.

One practical point may deserve mention. In all the letters to churches except—once more—Philadelphians, Ignatius speaks of those who "refresh" itinerant Christians. Indeed, with the verb "refresh" he always uses the expression "in every way." So the Ephesians and the Smyrnaeans refreshed Ignatius at Smyrna (Eph. 2:1; Magn. 15:1; Smyrn. 9:2), as did other churches (Trall. 12:1—"in flesh and in spirit"). The Smyrnaeans also refreshed Philo and Rheus Agathopous

(Smyrn. 10:1), and the Ephesian deacon Burrhus refreshed Ignatius (12:1). It is right for the Roman church to refresh Syrian prisoners (Rom. 10:2).

Rather clearly, this work of refreshment is equivalent to practical works of mercy of the kind which the Roman church was ready to provide for Ignatius, in this instance by preventing his martyrdom (Rom. 1:2ff.). Refreshment was not provided at Philadelphia, and, in imitation of Paul's words in 2 Corinthians 11:9, he states how glad he is that no one gave him support (Philad. 6:3). His gladness is not altogether complete, however, for in his view it is characteristic of the heterodox that they are not concerned with love in its practical application to widows, orphans, those in distress, prisoners and former prisoners, the hungry or the thirsty (Smyrn. 6:2).

With the exception of Romans, the letters are largely concerned with the problem created by the existence of heterodoxy in the various communities. It has been argued (e.g. by Bauer, 240) that Ignatius was basically opposing one heresy only, and that it had both Docetic and Judaistic aspects. In support of his view he claims that in Magnesians, primarily directed against Judaizers, there is anti-Docetic polemic, and refers to Magnesians 9:2; 11. Neither passage is necessarily aimed precisely at Magnesian heresy. Ignatius undoubtedly expressed antiheretical thoughts even when writing to communities like that of the Ephesians, among whom, he says, there is no heresy at all (6:2). It is more natural to assume that there were two distinct heresies, especially since Judaizing is discussed only in Magnesians and Philadelphians, Docetism only in Trallians and Smyrnaeans.

In Magnesians 8–11 Ignatius attacks those who wish to introduce or to maintain Jewish customs in the Christian Church. Apparently they appealed to the law of Moses, and against them Ignatius explains that the prophets lived "in accordance with Christ Jesus," for they no longer observed, or highly valued, the Sabbath (the same point is made, with a quotation from Isaiah 1:13, in Barnabas 15). Proof that the prophets expected Christ is provided by the statement that when he came, he raised them from the dead, presumably at his descent into Hades.[9] Ignatius insists that Judaism is the "old leaven" mentioned by Paul (1 Cor. 5:7) and that Christianity is not based on Judaism but that Judaism (because of the discipleship of the prophets) is based on Christianity. What is of cardinal importance is the birth, passion, and resurrection of Jesus Christ.

In Philadelphians 5–9 he makes similar points against his opponents and indicates that, as among the Galatians to whom Paul wrote, the Judaizers have made inroads among gentile Christians. Evidently at Philadelphia, as we have already seen, Ignatius encountered considerable hostility. There were those who denied that his knowledge of the local situation was given him by the Spirit; there were those who argued with him about the interpretation of Old Testament texts, presumably rejecting his view of the prophets as proto-Christians. He lays emphasis upon the supremacy of Jesus the High Priest over the Old Testament high priests and states that he is the one through whom patriarchs, prophets, apostles, and the Church have had access to God. The gospel about him is "the perfection of incorruption."

The Docetic heresy was maintained by those who held that Jesus merely "seemed" (dokein) to suffer. Ignatius does not state why they thought so, but when he speaks of his understanding of heavenly matters—such as "angelic locations and archontic conjunctions" (Trall. 5:2) or "the glory of the angels and the archons visible and invisible" (Smyrn. 6:1)—we may suppose that the context of their thought was to be found in semi-Gnostic speculations about spiritual powers. (Paul too opposes such speculations in Colossians.) Because of their concern for the spiritual, they could not believe in "the blood of Christ" (Smyrn. 6:1); that is to say, they could

[9] References in Bauer 227; see also W. Bieder, *Die Vorstellung von der Höllenfahrt Jesu Christi* (Zurich, 1949), 141-143.

not accept the reality of his suffering (Trall. 10:1; Smyrn. 2:1, 4:2). And therefore they could not believe that he was really born, really ate and drank, or was really raised from the dead. "They abstain from Eucharist and prayer because they do not acknowledge that the Eucharist is the flesh of our Savior Jesus Christ which suffered for our sins" (Smyrn. 7:1). Moreover, because such people do not believe in the reality of human existence, they cannot express either Christian faith or Christian love: they do not participate in any of the works of mercy which are characteristic of Christians (Smyrn. 6:2).

It is in the light of such situations as these that Ignatius insists upon the unity of the Church and its subordination to the bishop and other regular ministers. Obviously he does not envisage the possibility that bishops and others might advocate unorthodox doctrines or practices. In his mind, bishops obtain their offices "in the love of God the Father and the Lord Jesus Christ" (Philad. 1:1); they have been established throughout the world "in the purpose of Jesus Christ" (Eph. 3:2). Polycarp, the ideal bishop of Smyrna, is to "stand fast as a beaten anvil," to "take punishment and yet win" (Polyc. 3:1). Under such circumstances the best guarantee of both faith and love lies in the ministry established by the Holy Spirit (Philad. inscr.).

Ignatius and the Bible

It cannot be said that, at least in these letters, Ignatius made much use of the Old Testament. He used the formula "it is written" in making quotations from the book of Proverbs (3:34 in Eph. 5:3; 18:17 in Magn. 12). But—especially in arguing with the heterodox—he did not find exact quotations very satisfactory. At Philadelphia he was questioned about his Old Testament exegesis and then said that the true foundation of Christian faith is not the Old Testament as such but Jesus Christ, toward whom the Old Testament prophets were looking (Philad. 8:2, cf. 5:2, 9:2; Smyrn. 7:2). On the other hand, his letters do contain allusions to Old Testament texts, two from Isaiah (5:26 in Smyrn. 1:2; 52:5 in Trall. 8:2) and one from the Psalms (32:9 in Eph. 15:1).[10] Moreover, there seem to be traces of Wisdom 7:29f. and 18:14f. in Ephesians 19;[11] and O. Perler has shown that the influence of the Hellenistic Jewish homily known as 4 Maccabees pervades his writings.[12]

These facts show (1) that Ignatius knew more about the Old Testament, in its Hellenistic Jewish form, than would at first appear likely, and (2) that we cannot expect him to provide definite quotations from the books that he knows, often by heart. The circumstances of his journey through Asia Minor would seem to militate against much checking of references.

As for New Testament references, the point at which to begin is with the Pauline epistles, which Ignatius certainly knows; he can say to the Ephesians (12:2) that Paul makes mention of them "in every letter,"[13] and therefore he knows a collection of Pauline epistles. Among these, the most important is 1 Corinthians, with at least forty-six quotations or allusions; but there are also allusions to Romans, 2 Corinthians, Galatians, Ephesians, Philippians, Colossians, 1 Thessalonians, and possibly to 1 and 2 Timothy. The cumulative evidence for Ignatius' use of a collection of letters is excellent.

The nature of his Christian faith and the kind of "Paulinism" he exemplifies is clearly indicated by his preference for the practical-mystical 1 Corinthians, but we shall not trace through all the allusions to it. Instead, we shall consider only a few examples of his way of referring to it in his letters. Some of them, as might be expected, are clearer than others. There can be little doubt about a passage like this:

Why are we foolishly perishing, ignoring the gift which the

[10] Perhaps also Ps. 57:5 in Eph. 9:1; Isa. 66:18 in Magn. 10:3.
[11] A. Cabaniss in *Vigiliae Christianae* 10 (1956), 97-102.
[12] *Rivista di archeologia cristiana* 25 (1949), 47-72.
[13] On the translation see Bauer 212.

Lord has truly sent? My spirit is devoted to the cross, which
is a stumbling block to unbelievers but salvation and eternal
life to us. Where is the wise man? Where is the debater?
Where is the boasting of the so-called intelligent?

Here (Eph. 17:2–18:1) Ignatius is obviously following 1 Corinthians 1:18-20 with remarkable care. But he also quotes
isolated phrases from the epistle—for example, in Trallians
12:3 and in Romans 5:1.

I need your love, so that I may be judged worthy of the lot
which I am set to obtain, "lest I be found a castaway"
(1 Cor. 9:27).
I become more of a disciple because of their wrong doing,
"but not by this am I justified" (1 Cor. 4:4).

This is to say that he can take Pauline expressions and use
them in contexts of his own. Such usage is hardly surprising.
Ignatius, in fact, could not have used Pauline expressions in
Pauline contexts.

We should also point out that he feels quite free to para-
phrase Paul's words. According to 1 Corinthians 6:9-10, "the
unrighteous" will not inherit the kingdom of God; the unrighteous are defined as those who practice certain kinds of
sins. When Ignatius uses this passage he rewrites it, and in
several ways. In Ephesians 16:1 he paraphrases it thus: "Do
not be deceived, my brothers; those who corrupt families
(οἱ οἰκοφθόροι) will not inherit the kingdom of God." He is
laying emphasis upon only one of several points which Paul
was making, though upon the one which in the context of
1 Corinthians was the most important. In Philadelphians 3:3
he is concerned with another point: "Do not be deceived,
my brothers; whoever follows a schismatic will not inherit
the kingdom of God." Interestingly enough, these two paraphrases contain Ignatius' only references to the kingdom of
God. And he further paraphrases the second of them in this
way: "Whoever walks in accordance with an alien opinion is

not in agreement with the passion." The relation of passion and kingdom of God is ultimately based on synoptic doctrine about suffering as prior to Christ's entrance into glory (cf. Luke 24:26; Mark 10:37-40; etc.). What is significant here is that Ignatius does not restrict himself to Paul's words or to exact exegesis of what Paul said; he synthesizes New Testament teaching as he paraphrases.

He can also take Paul's words as referring to himself, as we have already seen. It may seem rather surprising that he can thus use words in which Paul speaks of himself as an apostle; but such is the case. In Ephesians 21:2 Ignatius speaks of himself as the last or least of the Syrian Christians judged worthy to serve for God's honor. This might seem to be a simple, straightforward statement. But in Magnesians 14 and Trallians 13:1 the thought recurs, expressed thus: "I am not worthy to be called a part of them [the Syrian Christians], since I am the least of them." The words "not worthy to be called" now show us that "least" is derived from 1 Corinthians 15:8, and in Romans 9:2 the word confirms the point. Here Ignatius is using what we may call "allusive quotation." Of course we cannot prove our point, but we should suggest that in every instance, not just the last, he had 1 Corinthians in mind.

Now what does this use of 1 Corinthians show? It shows that Ignatius used the letter in several different ways and that sometimes he quoted, sometimes he alluded, sometimes he allusively quoted and sometimes he quotingly alluded. Any idea of exactness in analyzing his usage must be read in by the analyst. It does not exist in Ignatius' own writings.

Now we turn to the question of the Gospels. Few topics have been more militantly debated, at least as far as Ignatian studies are concerned. It is hard to see why this has been so. Perhaps it has been felt that if Ignatius did not know Matthew and John, his letters could be regarded as unchristian or at any rate unbiblical. The most important recent

works on the subject are concerned with his use or nonuse of
Matthew and John.

In dealing with the synoptic tradition in the Apostolic
Fathers, Helmut Koester classifies the materials common to
Ignatius and to the synoptics (especially Matthew) in a
highly schematic way: "kerygmatic tradition," "mythological
expressions," "paraenetic formulas and similarities in terminology," "free tradition," and "special relationship with a
single gospel." By arranging the materials in this way he is
able to place last the passage that, one might suppose, would
go at the beginning of his study: Matthew 3:15 in relation
to Smyrnaeans 1:1 (Jesus was baptized by John "so that all
righteousness might be fulfilled by him"). But since Koester
has already disposed of all other echoes of Matthew, he can
now take care of Matthew 3:15 as well. Since Ignatius himself was interested only in the sacramental meaning of baptism, not in the problem to which Matthew refers, he would
not have read Matthew. "Would not have" soon becomes
"did not"; in Koester's view the passage in Smyrnaeans 1:1
reflects a kerygmatic formula composed by someone else—
who did read Matthew![14]

Again, there are two passages in Ignatius' letter to Polycarp
(2:1-2) which might suggest that he knew the Gospels.

If you love good disciples	If you love those who love you,
it is no credit to you.	what credit is it to you? (Luke 6:32)
Become wise (sing.)	Then become wise (pl.)
as a serpent in everything	as the serpents
and guileless forever	and guileless
as the dove.	as the doves (Matt. 10:16).

Here, one might suppose, is evidence for the use (presumably
from memory) of one Synoptic Gospel and then another
Synoptic Gospel. But no—the first quotation could have
arisen in the "free tradition" as a variant form of Matthew

[14] *Synoptische Überlieferungen bei den Apostolischen Vätern* (Berlin,
1957), 24-61.

5:46; and if this is so, then the second quotation could have come from "free tradition" too. Here Koester states his principle clearly: "It is more probable that both logia come from the free tradition than that one is derived from Matthew, the other from Luke."[15] Why is it more probable? Koester goes on to state that "today words of Jesus are adduced by men who have never read a gospel." Undoubtedly this is so. Is it relevant? Arguments of this kind make the use of texts unnecessary. The analogy controls the argument and provides the conclusion.

Let us try a different analogy. Modern New Testament critics would certainly avoid combining materials from various Gospels in the way in which (it would appear) Ignatius combined them. Was he a New Testament critic? Was he using books at the time he wrote his letters? Was he really concerned with keeping the Gospels separate?

Actually, in almost every case (except, we should hold, the ones cited above) it is possible to hold either that Ignatius was relying upon memories of what he had read (scripture) or that he was relying upon memories of what he had heard (oral tradition). To make a decision is very difficult. Analogies inevitably enter into consideration. The kind of memory ascribed to Ignatius tends to be the kind of memory possessed by the scholar discussing his work. Thus Koester would say that Ignatius had an excellent memory and used oral tradition; I should incline to say that his memory was not that exact and that he may have remembered books. (He certainly remembered a book in the case of 1 Corinthians.)

The relation between Ignatius and the Gospel of John has been discussed by Christian Maurer.[16] Probably the most important parallel is that between the Eucharistic passages in Ignatius and those in John. It seems hardly deniable that Ignatius' identification of "the bread of God" with "the flesh of Christ," and his mention of "drink" in the same context

[15] *Ibid.*, 43.
[16] *Ignatius von Antiochien und das Johannesevangelium* (Zurich, 1949).

(Rom. 7:3), is based upon John 6:33, 51, 55. Similarly, in
Smyrn. 7:1, Ignatius states that the Eucharist is the flesh
of our Savior Jesus Christ (on both passages see Maurer
34-40, 77-99). As secondary, though important, evidence one
may cite the description of the Spirit as knowing "whence
it comes and whither it goes" (Philad. 7:1; John 3:8; cf.
8:14; Maurer 25-30, 45-58), the mention of Jesus as "the
door to the Father" (Philad. 9:1; John 10:7, 9; 14:6; Maurer
30-34, 58-77), and the minor parallels which Maurer mentions (41-43).

But just as Ignatius never mentions any apostles except
Peter and Paul, and uses formulas of quotation only twice,
both in reference to the Old Testament, so in making use of
the Gospel of John he does not speak of its author or use it
in a consciously literary way. What he knows of John he
knows from memory; what he knows from memory is, so to
speak, written in his heart. He does not, and probably would
not if he could, make use of a book directly.

Indeed, it is possible, as W. J. Burghardt has suggested,
that he knows not the Gospel of John but its author.[17] Admittedly such a suggestion may seem shocking to literary
critics, accustomed to relations between documents but not
between people. Yet it remains possible that Ignatius had
actually known some of the apostles, even though everything
that has been transmitted on this subject is legend. It is
fairly probable that in the first century, even toward its end,
there were Christians whose Christianity had not come to
them through books.

Conceivably we are asking the wrong kind of question of
Ignatius. E. Flesseman-van Leer is surely right when she
states that "Ignatius attaches little importance to the authority of scripture as such (though he nowhere denies this
importance)."[18] In fact, we should be inclined to go a little

[17] *Theological Studies* 1 (1940), 156.
[18] *Tradition and Scripture in the Early Church* (Assen, Holland, 1954),
35.

beyond this conclusion and to suggest that for him apostolic doctrine, as interpreted in the Church (or as foreshadowed in the Old Testament), is of primary significance. It makes little difference to him whether the doctrine has been transmitted in oral or in written form. Because the matter is unimportant, it is hard to decide whether he is using written or oral sources at various points. Perhaps the best example of the difficulty is provided in Smyrnaeans 3:1-3.

> I know and believe that even after the resurrection he was in the flesh. And when he came to those with Peter he said, "Take, handle me and see that I am not an incorporeal demon." And immediately they touched him and believed, being mingled with his flesh and spirit. Therefore they despised death and were found to be above death. After the resurrection he ate and drank with them as a being of flesh, though spiritually he was united with the Father.

Where do the words ascribed to Jesus come from? According to Origen, they come from a *Doctrina Petri* (an inference from the mention of Peter here?); according to Jerome, from the Gospel According to the Hebrews. Eusebius says he does not know their source. There is no reason to suppose that any of these Fathers had considered Ignatius' manner of citation as carefully as modern scholars have done, and we therefore venture to suggest that Ignatius is simply paraphrasing Luke 24:39 ("Handle me and see, for a spirit does not have flesh and bones such as you see that I have")— especially since eating and drinking with the risen Lord is mentioned in Luke 24:30, 35, 41-43, as well as in Acts 10:41 (in a speech by Peter).

We should not regard it as absolutely impossible or unsuitable for Ignatius to have made use of an apocryphal gospel. But it seems just as likely that he was using Luke in the way in which, as we have seen, he used other written sources—from memory. Finally, we submit that the question of "scripture or tradition" is not as clear cut as it looks, when we are considering the writings of a Christian who almost certainly was not using books at the time he wrote, whether or not he had used them earlier. Under such circumstances, scripture would tend to be treated as tradition, just as at earlier points, even in Ignatius' lifetime, tradition almost certainly came to be crystallized as scripture.

III. Polycarp of Smyrna

A. The Letter or Letters to the Philippians

Polycarp, bishop of Smyrna early in the second century and a martyr there in 156 or 167, is one of the best-known personages among the early Christians. A correspondent of Ignatius of Antioch, he collected Ignatius' letters and later was the teacher of both Irenaeus and a Valentinian Gnostic named Florinus; he was martyred at an age in excess of eighty-six years. Simply because of his very long life and episcopate, he became a primary link between the subapostolic Church and the Church of a much later period. His existence and his writings stand on guard against attempts to claim that during the second century Christianity was completely transformed.

To or about Polycarp we possess the letters of Ignatius addressed to Smyrna, the martyr-acts of Polycarp, and the remarks of Irenaeus about him. From Polycarp himself comes the letter to the Philippians, in Greek preserved only in an eleventh-century manuscript (Cod. Vatic. Gr. 859) or in copies derived from it. This manuscript does not contain the whole letter, for which we have to turn to Eusebius (in part) and to the Latin version (the whole). In addition, there are a few quotations in Monophysite or semi-Monophysite writers of the fifth to the seventh centuries; these have some importance for the text, as we shall see.

It should be added that it is not altogether certain that the letter of Polycarp really is one letter. The basic difficulty lies in the fact that in Philippians 9:1-2, he clearly regards

Ignatius and other martyrs as dead, while in 13:2, unfortunately preserved only in Latin, he asks for news of Ignatius "and those who are with him" (*de his qui cum eo sunt*). Two possibilities are open: (1) It can be argued that the Latin is a mistranslation of the Greek, which lacked a verb; there is, in fact, a similar mistranslation in 9:1, where the Greek, verbless, clearly refers to dead martyrs from Philippi and the Latin translation wrongly reads not "among yourselves" but *qui ex vobis sunt*. (2) It can be argued that the translation is correct and that we have parts of two letters from Polycarp; this is the claim of P. N. Harrison in his *Polycarp's Two Epistles to the Philippians* (Cambridge, England, 1936). He suggested that the first letter, written in Ignatius' lifetime, consisted, as far as we know it, of chapters 13 and 14 of the present epistle, while chapters 1 through 12 come from a letter written considerably later and perhaps directed against Marcion, say about A.D. 135.

The absence of New Testament allusions or quotations in chapters 13 and 14 does not prove anything about the date of this letter, if it is a letter, for the subject matter simply does not require the presence of such allusions. On the other hand, the presence of countless allusions, and a few explicit quotations, in chapters 1 through 12, clearly shows that Polycarp has a collection of literature (including the Pastoral Epistles and probably 1 Clement) which he regards as authoritative and knows practically by heart.

What is it that he knows? There seem to be only two places in which there are implicit quotations from the Old Testament: "almsgiving sets free from death" (10:2; Tobit 4:10 and 12:9) and "Woe to him through whom the name of the Lord is blasphemed" (10:3; Isaiah 52:5 as quoted in 2 Clem. 13:2). Far more frequent are quotations from the New Testament books. Polycarp uses the formula "knowing that" as an introduction to four quotations:

1:3 Ephesians 2:5, 8, 9
4:1 1 Timothy 6:7

5:1 Galatians 6:7
6:1 "We are all debtors to sin" (Matt. 6:12[?]
Luke 11:4[?] Rom. 3:23[?])

He knows that Paul wrote letters to the Philippians (3:2; cf. 11:3) and can refer to the teaching of Paul (11:2; 1 Cor. 6:2). He can even quote Ephesians 4:26 from "the scriptures" (12:1).

He can also speak of "remembering what the Lord said when he taught" (2:3). This turns out to be a combination of gospel sayings somehow related to 1 Clement 13:1-2.

Polycarp	1 Clement	Gospels
Judge not, that you be not judged;	(As you judge, so you will be judged)	Matt. 7:1; Luke 6:37 (D, Marcion)
Forgive, and it will be forgiven you;	Forgive, so that it may be forgiven you;	different order
Pity, so that you may be pitied;	Pity, so that you may be pitied;	
With the measure you measure, it will be measured back to you;	With the measure you measure, by it it will be measured to you.	Matt. 7:2 (Mark 4:24)
Blessed are the poor and those persecuted for righteousness' sake, for theirs is the kingdom of God.		Luke 6:20 Matt. 5:10 Luke 6:20

It is clear that Polycarp is not relying *directly* upon either 1 Clement or the written Gospels. He is making use of his memory either in regard to such written documents or in regard to oral traditions; and it does not seem to be possible to tell which he is doing. But it is evident that he knows written epistles by Paul, as well as by Clement, and it remains possible that he knows written Gospels as well, not to mention 1 Peter and 1 John.

Polycarp's reliance upon traditional materials, oral or written, is so extensive as to justify thoroughly Eduard Norden's comments upon the letter(s).[19]

[19] *Die antike Kunstprosa* II (Leipzig, 1898), 512.

The language deserves neither praise nor blame; no unusual word, no anacoluthon—but also no original thought, no rhetoric either of heart or of head (e.g., there are no antitheses).

The document is so thoroughly "traditional" as to have provoked an occasional suspicion that Polycarp cannot have written it. But everything we know of Polycarp suggests that he was just the sort of person who would have created such a literary expression—if we can use the word "create."

Scholars have often pointed out that most of what Polycarp wrote can be regarded as a mosaic of quotations, and it is this fact which lent a measure of plausibility to the theory of J. M. Cotterill, that another mosaic creator, the seventh-century monk Antiochus, not only quoted from the letter but actually wrote it.[20] The details of Cotterill's argument are not very convincing, however, and we may still assume that Polycarp wrote the letter or letters ascribed to him and quoted by Eusebius.

The mosaic of Polycarp possesses its own interest, partly because it seems to reflect all the Pauline epistles but Philemon, as well as 1 or 2 John, 1 Peter, 1 Clement, some of the Ignatian letters, synoptic traditions, and perhaps Acts, James, and Hermas. More important is the question as to which sources he used most frequently and significantly. As for frequency, Polycarp made use of 1 Peter at least eighteen times and 1 Clement fifteen times. Allusions to these documents are much more common than allusions to any other writings—although if we were to treat the Pauline epistles as a group, allusions to it occur forty-one times (including thirteen allusions to the Pastorals). As for significance, Polycarp echoes Paul's letter to the Philippians as he writes to the same community; and when he speaks of Paul as having written "letters" (3:2) to them, he may also have 2 Thessalonians in mind (11:3).[21] When he attacks heresy,

---

[20] *Journal of Philology* 19 (1891), 241-285.
[21] Cf. E. Schweizer in *Theologische Zeitschrift* 1 (1945), 90-91.

he uses the language of the Johannine epistles (7:1; 1 John
4:2-3; 2 John 7). As A. E. Brooke wrote, "The passage may
be said to *prove* the acquaintance of Polycarp with the teaching contained in the Epistles, or with the man who taught
it."[22] Finally, there are, as we might expect, allusions to the
letters which Ignatius wrote from and to Smyrna.[23]

What is interesting about Polycarp's letter itself? As far
as one can see, the only novel, or relatively novel, feature
in his thought is to be found in a rather obscure passage or
two in chapter 12. Here there are a couple of textual variants
which point toward a Christology more like that of Ignatius
than like the more Jewish of the Apostolic Fathers. "May the
God and Father of our Lord Jesus Christ, and the eternal
High Priest himself, God Jesus Christ"—such is the way one
passage begins, at least according to some of the Latin manuscripts. Similarly, there is a later reference to "those who
will believe in our Lord and God Jesus Christ and in his
Father." In each case some manuscripts, though not the ones
which Diekamp regards as the best, contain readings in
which a "lower" Christology is expressed.

On what basis can one defend the higher Christology readings? Here one must remember that the manuscripts of the
Latin Polycarp are manuscripts which contain the Latin
Pseudo-Ignatius, in which the Christology of Ignatius himself has been "lowered." Is it not possible that the manuscripts in which a low Christology is ascribed to Polycarp
have been edited for that purpose, and that his authentic
Christology was not too different from that of his hero
Ignatius?

The high priesthood of Christ is clearly stated in the prayer
which the martyr Polycarp uttered before his death (Mart.
14:3), but Christ is described not as God but as "Child" (an
expression characteristic of early Christian prayers). On the

[22] *The Johannine Epistles* (London, 1912), liii.
[23] Eph. 7:1 (6:3), 10:3 (8:2), 11:2 (1:1); ?Trall. 3:1 (5:2); Rom. 6:1
(9:2), ?10:1-2 (13:2); Smyrn. 4:2 (9:2), 11:3 (13:1); Polyc. 8:1 (13:1).

other hand, the doxology of the prayer clearly suggests that the Child is God, for it reads "through whom be glory to thee with him and the Holy Spirit." Armitage Robinson thought that this doxology, shared with the Ethiopic Church, showed that the Martyrdom came from a time after the second century; but this is by no means certain.[24]

B. The Martyrdom of Polycarp

We know more about Polycarp than what we can derive from his letter, for Irenaeus, who wrote late in the second century, had known him personally, and we also possess an account of his martyrdom in a letter sent by "the Church of God which sojourns in Smyrna" to "the Church of God which sojourns in Philomelium"—a town in Phrygia—and to "all the sojournings of the Holy Catholic Church in every place."[25] This letter was known to, and used by, Eusebius, early in the fourth century, in his *Church History* (4, 15), and it survives separately in six Greek manuscripts and a Latin translation.

The document begins with a mention of the similarity of Polycarp's sufferings to those of Christ, and then a description of the other martyrs of the time. After a young man named Germanicus insisted, like Ignatius (Rom. 5:2), upon being killed by a wild beast, the crowd at the arena demanded a search for Polycarp, who, as the aged bishop of Smyrna, was devoting himself to prayer for the churches. When he was brought into the city and into the arena, the Roman proconsul tried to persuade him to recant, but when he refused, he was burned alive. The account ends with the praises of Polycarp, with instructions about transmitting the letter, with a doxology, and with a personal greeting from the scribe (Mart. 19–20). In the manuscript several notes have been added: a confusing note about the date of the

[24] *Journal of Theological Studies* 21 (1919-20), 97-105.
[25] The word "sojourning" (*paroikia*) is the source of the modern "parish."

martyrdom, a final salutation, and a statement about the translation of the text.

> Gaius copied this from the text of Irenaeus, the disciple of Polycarp, and he lived with Irenaeus. I, Socrates, wrote it down in Corinth, copying the text of Gaius. Grace be with all. And I, Pionius, wrote it down from the previous copy after searching for it after the blessed Polycarp revealed it to me in a vision.

These remarks are very explicit but, unfortunately, not wholly trustworthy. It is by no means certain that Pionius, a martyr in the Decian persecution, was actually concerned with the life and death of Polycarp, although a fourth-century *Life of Polycarp* presents itself as having been written by him. In this *Life of Polycarp* we find a similar concern for old manuscripts; the visit of Paul to Smyrna—to ordain Polycarp—is "as I have found it in ancient copies" (ch. 1). It is fairly likely that the Martyrdom of Polycarp is more reliable than the remarks about the way in which it was transmitted; the *Life of Polycarp*, less so. In both cases the words about manuscripts were added when a kind of *corpus Polycarpianum* was created. (We should add that we are not here discussing the *Life of Polycarp* because it casts no light whatever on the historical person; it is a bit of edifying fiction from the fourth century.)

In discussing the doxology of the prayer in the Martyrdom of Polycarp (ch. 14), J. A. Robinson, as we said, suggested that the Martyrdom did not come from the second century. A more thoroughgoing analysis of the document was provided by H. von Campenhausen in the *Sitzungsberichte* of the Heidelberg Academy for 1957. His point of departure is to be found in the differences between the version of the Martyrdom provided in the manuscripts and the version set forth in the *Church History* of Eusebius (4, 15, 3-14). In von Campenhausen's view the passages not to be found in

Eusebius come largely from a "gospel-type revision," whose author tried to make Polycarp's martyrdom as close as possible to that of Jesus. But since the same purpose is reflected in some passages to which Eusebius *does* refer, we should have to think of the Martyrdom as undergoing a whole series of interpolations and revisions, not just one. In von Campenhausen's view this is what happened. But it is by no means certain that the absence of a passage from Eusebius proves that it was not in the document from which Eusebius was quoting; and the absence of one type of passage (among others) from Eusebius does not prove that passages of the same type present in his version are interpolations.

I should incline to agree with von Campenhausen (and others) that chapters 20–21 were added at a later date. I should not agree that he has proved the existence of various other additions.

The date of Polycarp's martyrdom, once regarded as firmly fixed by the calculations of C. H. Turner and E. Schwartz, who set it precisely on February 22, A.D. 156, has become unsettled in recent times by those who regard the chronology in chapter 21 as due to a late editor. Eusebius, who knew the Martyrdom with or without this chronological chapter, did not hesitate to date the event in 166-167. To a considerable extent we ought to rely on a series of judgments based on Ignatius' letters to the Smyrnaeans and to Polycarp. If Polycarp died in 156, he was about thirty when Ignatius wrote him; if he died a decade later, he was obviously about forty. Equally obviously, it is hard to make guesses based on the tone of Ignatius as he writes about, or to, Polycarp; but I venture to think that it is more appropriate in relation to a young bishop than in relation to a somewhat older one.

IV. The Didache

The Didache, or Teaching of the Twelve Apostles, or Teaching of the Lord through the Twelve Apostles to the

gentiles, begins with a description of the "two ways" of life
and death (1:1–2:7). The way of life is based on the great
commandments of the Gospel, on the counsels of perfection
in the Sermon on the Mount (especially those related to
charitable giving), and on the last five of the Ten Commandments. Next comes a little moral homily based on the pattern,
"My child, do not be (adjective describing a person), for
(cognate noun referring to a vice) leads to (something
worse); (something worse) comes from all these" (ch. 3).
Further moral discussion concludes the way of life (ch. 4);
the way of death is then briefly described (ch. 5). The reader
is advised to "bear the yoke of the Lord" (equivalent to the
way of life) insofar as he is able to do so; if he bears all of it,
he will be perfect. He should observe dietary laws—not
previously mentioned—as far as possible but should abstain
absolutely from meats offered to idols (6:3).

At the beginning of chapter 7, the point of what has been
mentioned hitherto becomes clearer. It is related to Christian
baptism. The statement about the two ways is to be used as a
preliminary catechism, and then the candidate is to be baptized in the name of the Father and of the Son and of the
Holy Spirit. Running water is preferable but not essential;
cold water is better than warm. If quantities of water are
not available—sufficient for immersion, presumably—water
can be poured three times on the candidate's head. The
baptizer and the one baptized are to fast before baptism;
the one baptized, for one or two days.

Mention of fasting in chapter 7 logically leads to a discussion of fasting and prayer. First the gospel saying about
not fasting as the hypocrites do (cf. Matt. 6:16) is trans-
muted into a novel statement: "Do not let your fasts take
place with the hypocrites" (8:1); and on the basis of this
transformation, novel exegesis is provided. Hypocrites, i.e.,
observant Jews, fast on the second and fifth days of the week
(Mondays and Thursdays); Christians should therefore fast
on Wednesdays and "preparations" (the Jewish name for

Friday; cf. John 19:31). The words resemble Matthew 6:16; the content is quite different, for "hypocrisy" is something the Didachist does not seem to understand. Again, Christians are not to pray as the hypocrites do but "as the Lord commanded in his gospel," using the Lord's Prayer three times a day (8:2-3). Again, the words are like those of Matthew 6:5 ff., but the Didachist has lost the meaning.

At this point the central section of the Didache begins, it contains prayers for use before and after the Eucharistic meal (chs. 9-10). The prayers are close to Jewish table blessings of the time, as M. Dibelius demonstrated. Structurally the three prayers (for the cup, for the broken bread, after eating) are essentially the same. Each begins with "We give thanks to thee for what thou hast made known to us through thy child Jesus; to thee be glory forever." The prayer over the cup ends here, for it is to be followed immediately by the prayer over the broken bread. The prayer over the bread compares the unity of the loaf, made from scattered grain, with the future unity of the Church in God's kingdom; similarly, the prayer after eating briefly refers to God's gift of food and drink both material and spiritual and then speaks of the gathering of the Church into the kingdom. Brief interjections conclude the form.

> Let grace come and this world pass away.
> Hosanna to the God of David.
> If anyone is holy, let him come;
> if anyone is not, let him repent.
> Maranatha. Amen.

The prophets (not previously mentioned) are free not to use this form.

One of the most thoroughgoing analyses for any of the Apostolic Fathers is that which J. P. Audet has provided for the Didache.[26] In his view the present document came into existence through processes which can definitely be re-

[26] *La Didaché: instructions des apôtres* (Paris, 1958).

constructed. The earliest Didache consisted of 1:1-3a, 2:2–
5:2; 7:1; and 8:1–11:2. It ended here because Nicephorus of
Constantinople, listing the Didache among the New Testament apocrypha, says it was 200 lines long,[27] and lines often
included about 36 letters each. Two hundred lines would
lead to Didache 11:3 (though one would have to count all
the passages which Audet has just excluded).

Later the same author, probably an apostle, wrote Didache
11:3–13:2 and 14:1–16:8. In the interval, the Gospel of
Matthew appeared; in the first part of the Didache it is not
mentioned as a book. Afterward, additions were made by
someone else: Didache 1:3b–2:1a; 6:2-3; 7:2-4; and 13:3-7.
Last of all came two interpolations: the first sentence of 1:4
and the whole of 13:4.

Obviously this theory about the Didache is based primarily on internal, not external, evidence. It is interesting
that Nicephorus thought the Didache was 200 lines long,
but there is little reason to suppose that he knew the first
ten chapters or so. It is hard to be sure that the passages
Audet calls later additions were added by someone not the
author of the book.

The question of the use of biblical sources in the Didache
is remarkably difficult to answer, and remarkably different
answers have been provided. On the one hand, S. E. Johnson
has argued that the Didache represents an expansion of the
Gospel of Matthew, especially of Matthew 28:19-20: "Go,
make disciples of all the nations [or gentiles], baptizing them
into the Name of the Father and the Son and the Holy Spirit,
teaching them to observe everything which I have commanded you. . . ."[28] This kind of baptism is discussed in
chapter 7; the "way of the teaching" is to be found, in
catechetical form, in chapters 1 through 6; and liturgical
instructions based on Matthew 6 occur in chapter 8. To these
materials the Didachist has added liturgical models (chs. 9–

[27] *Ibid.*, 88-90.
[28] *Munera Studiosa W. H. P. Hatch* (Cambridge, Mass., 1946), 107-122.

10), advice on church life (chs. 11–15), and an apocalypse based on Matthew 24. On the other hand, H. Koester has subjected the alleged quotations from, or allusions to, Matthew to the solvent of individual analysis, with the conclusion that the Didachist's primary source was the oral tradition. He admits, however, that he knew Matthew and Luke, though he sees traces of them only in Didache 1:3-5.[29]

Apart from these Gospels—which, as Koester rightly notes, he did not use as "scripture"—the Didachist quotes directly only from Malachi (1:11, 14 in 14:3), from Zechariah (14:5 in 16:7), and apparently from Sirach (12:1, 7:22 in 1:6).[30] Frequent allusions to Sirach in various parts of the Didache point toward the Jewish-Christian origin of its author.[31]

As for the date and provenance of the Didache, there is the usual ambiguity. It obviously comes from a rather conservative Jewish-Christian community, but the very word "conservative" indicates that its date is not easy to fix. If its counsel to appoint bishops and deacons for the ministry of the prophets and teachers (15:1) is historically authentic, it probably comes from the late first century, for in the early second century Ignatius could write—with or without exaggeration—that bishops had been appointed throughout the world (Eph. 3:2). Some scholars have held that it is a Montanist or an anti-Montanist production or an orthodox forgery of the late second century, but the evidence adduced in support of such views is not altogether convincing.

It has been regarded as Egyptian because of its use as scripture by Clement of Alexandria, but its incorporation into the Syrian *Didascalia apostolorum* is probably more important. We should incline to agree with those who have treated the Didache as a representative of Syrian Christi-

[29] *Synoptische Überlieferungen bei den Apostolischen Vätern* (*Texte und Untersuchungen* 65, Berlin, 1957), 159-241.

[30] See C. H. Turner in *Journal of Theological Studies* 7 (1905-6), 593-595.

[31] Sir. 4:5 (4:8), 4:36 (4:5), 7:22 (1:6), 7:30 (1:2), 7:31-32 (13:3), 8:1 (1:4), 12:1 (1:6). All but three of these come from sections which Audet regards as additions to the original.

anity, though probably not from Antioch, in view of the
neglect of it by Ignatius and Theophilus, bishops in that city.

V. The Epistle of Barnabas

The content of the Epistle of Barnabas is in essence rather
simple. The author begins by laying emphasis on three
doctrines of the Lord: the hope of life, righteousness, and
love of joy and gladness (1:6). The main part of his book,
however, has practically nothing to do with these subjects
but is devoted to a critical analysis of the Old Testament
law, which "the wretched men" (16:1) did not understand.
The themes mentioned by Barnabas are precisely those which
the later Ebionites, hostile to Judaism, were to develop.

God is really opposed to sacrifices (2:4-10), which were
replaced by the sacrifice of Jesus (8:1-7; 12). He is opposed
to fasting and the scapegoat (3:1-5), for the true scapegoat
is Jesus (7:3-11). Circumcision (ch. 9) has been replaced by
baptism (ch. 11), and Moses' dietary laws really refer to
moral questions (ch. 10). The Sabbath has been replaced by
the Christians' eighth day (ch. 15), and the Jewish temple
by the presence of God in believers (ch. 16).

After a brief transition (ch. 17), Barnabas turns to the two
ways of light and darkness (chs. 18–20) and a final warning
(ch. 21). His concluding sections are based either on the
"two ways" of the Didache (chs. 1–6) or on a common source.

It is difficult to make much sense out of the arrangement
Barnabas has given his materials. Though he has a definite
introduction and an equally definite conclusion (in fact, two
of them, in chs. 17 and 21), the fact that the bulk of his book
is essentially a collection of proof texts does not make it easy
to read. In an important recent study, P. Prigent has tried
to differentiate three kinds of materials, most of them derived from Jewish sources.[32] These are (1) texts useful for

---

[32] *L'épître de Barnabe et ses sources* (Paris, 1961); see the review by R.
A. Kraft in *Journal of Theological Studies* 13 (1962), 401-408.

anticultic polemic, (2) Jewish midrashic traditions, and (3) messianic texts. In the first group he includes arguments against sacrifices and fasting, circumcision, the continuation of the Jewish covenant, and the Jewish temple. The midrashic traditions include discussions of paradise and the promised land as prefigurations of baptism, of the Day of Atonement and the sacrifice of a heifer, of prefigurations of the cross and of Jesus, and arguments to show that Christians have inherited the covenant. The messianic texts, of course, are taken as pointing to Christ.

The anticultic ideas could be found within Judaism, as various scholars have pointed out, and they are expressed in a different way, in Barnabas' time, in the semi-Gnostic Gospel of Thomas, where fasting, prayer, almsgiving, circumcision, dietary laws, and the temple are all rejected.[33] Prigent treats Barnabas' rejection of the dietary laws as belonging to the "midrashic traditions," but perhaps it goes with the anticultic texts.

In Barnabas' opinion the true, permanently valid Old Testament law is the Decalogue—a point which may suggest that he comes from Syria, where this view was held, though one cannot always locate ideas on a map. One of the most interesting features of the Epistle of Barnabas is its quotations from what is called scripture. Naturally enough, scripture includes the law, the prophets, and the writings, though all three parts are ascribed to prophets (cf. 6:8; 6:4). But the "canon" of Barnabas is not restricted to these materials. (1) A passage from 1 Enoch 89 is paraphrased in Barnabas 4:3, and ascribed to Enoch; in Barnabas 16:5 there is a direct quotation from the same passage, introduced with the words, "The scripture says." (2) In chapter 11 there is a collection of passages from various "prophets" (Jeremiah, Isaiah, Psalms, Ezekiel). Before the quotation from Ezekiel, and in Barnabas' mind apparently part of it, there is a quotation

[33] Prigent, *op. cit.*, 144.

from "another prophet," and this is 2 Baruch 61:7. (3) After
the quotation from Ezekiel, in chapter 12 we find another
"another prophet"—this time, 2 Esdras (4 Ezra) 4:33 and
5:5. (4) Finally, in Barnabas 4:14 the audience is urged to
pay attention "lest as it is written we be found 'many called
but few chosen' "—a reference to Matthew 20:16 and 22:14.
There is a clear allusion to the synoptic tradition or a synoptic
Gospel in Barnabas 5:9: "He came not to call the righteous
but sinners" (Matt. 9:13 and parallels); perhaps there is
another in 7:3: "When he was crucified he was given vinegar
and gall to drink" (Matt. 27:34, 48).

This means that insofar as Barnabas has a canon of
scriptural writings, it must include not only examples of the
Apocrypha and Pseudepigrapha of the Old Testament but
also at least one New Testament book—Matthew.

The date and provenance of Barnabas are equally difficult
to determine. Almost certainly the letter belongs to the
second century, not the first, for quotations from the Jewish
apocalyptic books 2 Baruch and 2 Esdras are ascribed to
prophets like Old Testament prophets (11:9; 12:1), and
these apocalypses come from the late first century or the
early second. It is possible, but most uncertain, that a reference to the destruction of the temple "by the enemies" and
to the temple's future rebuilding by "the servants of the
enemies" (16:4) has to do with the Roman attempt to re-
build the temple at Jerusalem in the year 131. If the reference were more precise, we could date Barnabas in 131
or 132; unfortunately, it is not so precise.

Again, we cannot be sure where Barnabas wrote. The fact
that his text of Isaiah is close to that used by Irenaeus[34]
might suggest that he wrote at Rome or in Asia Minor, but
the evidence is too tenuous for us to rely on it. A better clue
is probably provided by the use of the book as scripture by

[34] Cf. L.-M. Froidevaux in *Recherches de science religieuse* 44 (1956),
408-421.

Clement and Origen. This usage points toward an Alexandrian origin, since there are no traces of Barnabas in the second and third centuries outside Alexandria.[35]

VI.   The Shepherd of Hermas

The Shepherd begins with five visions, the first of which introduces not only Hermas and Rhoda (who rebukes him from heaven for having desired her) but also an aged woman in shining clothing with a book in her hand, seated on a chair of white wool; she reassures Hermas by telling him that his sins are due to his family, and then reads to him from the book before being taken away to the East. A year later he is on his way to Cumae, and the Spirit takes him to the scene of his previous vision. The aged lady appears and gives him the book to copy; a fortnight later he is able to understand the writing, and he learns that his wife is now to be like a sister to him, while for Christians in general there is to be reformation. Sins committed "up to this day" are to be forgiven, but later sinning will result in exclusion from salvation. Hermas learns that the aged lady is not, as he supposed, the Sibyl; she is the Church, old because pre-existent. She tells him to record her words in books to be sent to Clement and Grapte. The third vision is a vision of a tower "being built on the water with shining square stones"; the tower itself is the Church, built on the water "because your life was saved and will be saved through water" (i.e., baptism). The tower, "founded by the utterance of the almighty and glorious Name, is maintained by the invisible power of the Master" and is being completed by six archangels and by many other angels of God. The stones of the tower are apostles, bishops, teachers, deacons, and other saints. Seven women support it: they are faith, continence, simplicity, knowledge, innocence, reverence, and love. The

[35] Barnabas' relation to Antioch or Syria is not very close, as we have already suggested.

account ends with the statement that the aged lady seemed
to Hermas to grow younger, vision by vision; this was because
of his own increasing insight. Twenty days later Hermas saw
the fourth vision, on the Via Campana. A beast a hundred
feet long came toward him but did not attack him; after he
had gone thirty feet farther, the Church, even younger than
before, appeared to him and told him he had escaped because he had fearlessly confronted the beast. On its head
the beast had four colors: black for this world, red for the
impending blood and fire, gold for Hermas himself and other
Christians, and white for the age to come.

The fifth vision introduces the Shepherd, the angel of repentance, who informs Hermas that he is going to remain
with him and to give him commandments and parables;
Hermas is to write them down. Thus the Mandates begin.

The first is to believe that God is one; he is the absolute
creator and container of all. One must maintain faith, fear,
and continence. The second commends simplicity and innocence, especially in relation to almsgiving. The third is to
love truth; Hermas says that he himself has never spoken
a true word, and the angel urges him to change his ways.
The fourth deals with purity and avoiding thoughts of fornication and adultery; more practically, it is concerned with
adultery and forgiveness. Some teachers, Hermas continues
in a more general way, have said that postbaptismal sin cannot be forgiven; the angel explains that one occasion of forgiveness will be provided. The fifth cautions against "ill-
temper" (as Lake translates it); it is "foolish, frivolous, and
silly" and leads to bitterness, wrath, rage, and fury. The
sixth, seventh, and perhaps eighth explain what was meant
by faith, fear, and continence in the first Mandate. The
ninth, close in sentiment to the letter of James (1:7-8), rejects "double-mindedness"; the tenth rejects her "sister,"
grief. The eleventh warns against false prophets and teachers,
not inspired by the Holy Spirit. And the twelfth opposes evil
desire but favors good desire, thus closely paralleling the

rabbinic teaching about the good and evil impulses. All these commandments are easy if one has the Lord in his heart.

The ten Similitudes that follow have no introduction; the Shepherd simply continues speaking to Hermas in a somewhat allegorical style. The first parable describes the life of "resident aliens" who must remember to respect the laws of their own city if they wish to return to it. The second discusses the meaning of the fruitful vine growing upon the sterile elm tree; this means that the rich must support the poor while the poor pray for the rich. The third compares men with leafless trees; the significance of the comparison is that in the winter (the world) righteous and sinners look alike. In the fourth parable the thought is carried a little further: "Be fruitful so that your fruit may be known in the summer." These four parables are quite short, but the rest of Hermas' creations are considerably longer, and contain most of his theological ideas.

The fifth parable has a liturgical setting. Hermas is fasting, because he has a "station"—a military term used by Latin Christians in regard to a fixed time for the fast. The shepherd appears and says that fasting is often useless; godly conduct is more important and can be called a "great fast"; it leads to "living to God." The Shepherd then proceeds with the parable. A slave is told to fence a vineyard, not to do any more work with it. Actually, he proceeds to weed it during the master's absence. The result is that the master first frees the slave and then plans to make him joint heir with his son. As a token of his esteem, he sends him food from a feast. The servant shows his goodness by distributing much of the food among his fellow slaves, who pray for him, "that he might find greater favor with his master."

The Shepherd provides Hermas with two interpretations of this parable. The first, and the simpler of them, is practical. When you fast, figure out the difference between what you would normally consume and the bread and water you actually take; give this difference "to a widow or an orphan

or to someone in need." The second, reluctantly supplied by
the angel, gives symbolic equivalents for various details in
the story. As in a parable explanation in Matthew 13:38, the
field is the world. The master is God; the slave is his Son.
The vines are the people planted by God; the fences are
angels; the weeds are iniquities of God's slaves. The food
sent to the slave is the commandments given the people
through the Son. Hermas expresses his astonishment upon
hearing this explanation: "Everything is great and marvelous
and glorious." He does not understand, however, why the
Son has the form of a slave. It then develops that the Son
and the slave are not absolutely identical. Hermas' point
seems to be more moral than theological. He is concerned
with explaining that "all flesh in which the Holy Spirit has
dwelt will receive a reward," not with working out precise
Christological details.

The sixth parable is relatively brief, but it is important
because it introduces a series of parables based upon visions,
not upon stories. From this point to the end of the parables,
it would appear that Hermas took more care with his writing.
In extent, the first five parables are about as long as the next
three, while the last two are as long as the first eight. The
sixth parable tells of two shepherds and the state of their
sheep. The first shepherd, joyfully feeding his sheep well, is
the angel of luxury and deceit. There is, however, another
shepherd, savage and bitter, who is receiving the sheep
from the other one and placing them in a mountainous area
full of thorns and thistles; he is the angel of punishment. The
punishments—for whatever a man does with pleasure—last
360 times as long as the pleasures for which they are imposed.

The seventh parable deals with the same subject. Hermas
asks the Shepherd to ask the angel of punishment to leave
him; the affliction is too great. The Shepherd replies that he is
being punished for his family's sins; the head of the house
must suffer for them, even though they have repented.

The eighth parable is a complicated allegory about a

willow tree from which an angel cuts little sticks, giving them to "those called by the name of the Lord," who have gathered beneath the branches. Later the angel asks the people to give back the sticks, and they are returned in various states, ranging from dry and moth-eaten to green and bearing some fruit. The tree is interpreted as God's law, given to all the world, and identified as God's Son. The angel is Michael. The sticks too constitute the law, while the conditions in which they are returned are equivalent to apostasy or repentance. Those who walk in God's commandments will live to God.

The ninth parable is by far the longest, and it constitutes more than a quarter of the whole Shepherd of Hermas, half of the Similitudes. It is introduced by a promise at the end of the eighth: "And the rest I will show you after a few days." The Shepherd now summarizes Hermas' progress in strength and understanding; he is ready to learn about what he has seen from "the Holy Spirit which spoke . . . in the form of the Church . . . for that Spirit is the Son of God." The Shepherd then takes Hermas away to Arcadia, to a mountain on a plain surrounded by twelve mountains with various aspects. In the middle of the plain is a great white rock, with a "gate" or door cut in it; the door is surrounded by twelve virgins. Then six men come (obviously, as before, angels), accompanied by others, and they proceed to build a tower on the rock. Its foundations have four tiers, constructed out of ten, twenty (twenty-five), thirty-five, and forty stones. The tower is not completed, however, until the lord of the tower comes to test the stones, accepting some and replacing others. The stones rejected are taken away by twelve women, beautiful but savage.

Finally, after Hermas has had various conversations with the virgins, the Shepherd comes and explains what all this means. The rock and the gate in it is the Son of God, as is the lord who comes to test the stones. The tower is the

Church; the virgins are twelve virtues, while the women later mentioned are twelve vices. As for the mysterious foundation stones, the ten are the first generation, the twenty (twenty-five) the second generation of righteous men; the thirty-five are the prophets of God and his servants (deacons?), while the forty are apostles and teachers of the preaching of the Son of God. The twelve mountains around the plain are twelve nations of the world, or different kinds of persons.

The tenth parable is really simply an epilogue, counseling obedience to the commandments. Hermas' work is finished, and the book comes to a rather tranquil end without any clear conclusion.

As for Hermas' acquaintance with the biblical books or with pseudepigraphical literature, it is a striking fact that he refers only to one such work (Vis. 2, 3, 4)—and this is the book of Eldad and Modat, now lost. The Shepherd is full of what seem to be allusions to Old Testament passages, and even a few from the New Testament, but there are no exact quotations. Koester has denied that there are any passages at all which can clearly be traced to the Gospels,[36] but it is possible that in the elaborate Ninth Similitude a few occur. For instance, the rich "will enter the kingdom of God with difficulty" (9, 20, 2; Matt. 19:23) and those who are like infants will live in the kingdom of God (9, 29, 2; Matt. 18:3). But as Koester points out, the phrase in Matthew is "kingdom of heaven," and we must admit that Hermas may well have known nothing but oral tradition—unless perhaps (unlike the other Apostolic Fathers) he knew Mark (10:23, 25; 10:13-16).

Joly has laid emphasis on twelve passages in which Hermas is close to 2 Esdras, but all but two of these involve the apocalyptic form, not its substance. The two remaining instances show only that Hermas was making use of Jewish

[36] *Op. cit.*, 242-56.

apocalyptic ideas: the world was made for the people of God
(Vis. 2, 4, 1) and either Zion or the Church can be described
as a woman who appears in a vision (Vis. 3, 3, 3).

There is no question about the Roman origin of Hermas.
The date, however, is problematic. According to the Mura-
torian list (late second century) the Shepherd was written
"quite recently, in our own time in the city of Rome, by
Hermas, while his brother Pius was occupying the episcopal
throne of the church of the city of Rome." Joly accepts this
date—about 140—but does not explain how Pius could be
bishop of Rome if presbyters and bishops were practically
identical and those called presbyters governed the church.

In an important study entitled *Hermas et les Pasteurs*
(Paris, 1963), Stanislas Giet has endeavored to clear up
the difficulties in the *Shepherd* by ascribing it to three different authors. The first, Hermas himself, wrote the first four
Visions during the reign of Trajan (we may add that the
emphasis on one occasion for repentance reminds us of the
Syrian Gnostic Elchasai, who announced a similar opportunity in the third year of Trajan's reign). The second wrote
the ninth parable at a rather later date. The third, a Jewish
Christian like Hermas, composed the rest of the materials
(Vis. 5, Mandates, Sim. 1-8 and 10) about 160 to 170. In
spite of Giet's careful argumentation and his many incisive
comments, it remains probable that one author wrote the
work, and that none of it need be dated much later than 140.[37]

VII. Papias

One more Apostolic Father remains to be discussed: Papias
of Hierapolis, a small town in southwest Phrygia, just north
of Laodicea and Colossae. The reason we include him in this
group is that, according to Eusebius, he was a contemporary
of Polycarp—though in view of Polycarp's long life this means
no more than that he flourished during the first half of the

[37] See my review in *Gnomon* 36 (1964).

second century. His statements about tradition, however, suggest that he wrote at a time nearer A.D. 100 than 150.

Papias wrote five boks of Exegeses of the Dominical Oracles, and they seem to have been preserved at least until the fifth century, although it is hard to tell whether late writers are quoting from Papias or from those who had earlier read his books. Few theologians regarded him as significant, and Eusebius considered him stupid. The chief reason for this attitude seems to lie in Papias' emphasis upon, and frequent use of, uncontrolled oral tradition rather than authorized books. One tradition quoted by Irenaeus (Adv. haer. 5, 33, 3-4) is identical with what we read in the Jewish apocalyptic book 2 Baruch (29:4-8), though Papias ascribes it to Jesus. Eusebius says that he told strange miracle stories and parables (H. E. 3, 39, 8-11). In addition, he seems to have provided exegesis of the creation story, referring it to Christ and the Church.

Papias is an important witness to the existence of Jewish Christianity, although the fragments preserved by Eusebius deal primarily with Christian traditions and the books in which they were recorded. The loss of the Exegeses means that our picture of the Apostolic Fathers is less complete than it should be.

As for Papias' sources in addition to oral tradition, he certainly knew the Gospel of Mark, which he described as having been written by an "interpreter" of Peter, though not in order—possibly as compared with the order of the Gospel of John. He also states that Matthew compiled "the oracles" in a Hebrew dialect (either Hebrew or Aramaic), and that several Greek translations were in existence. We do not know whether or not he had read 2 Baruch. He must have read much of the Old Testament, but we do not know exactly what parts he had read. According to Eusebius he knew 1 Peter and 1 John.

Chapter IV

THE HISTORICAL CIRCUMSTANCES
OF THE APOSTOLIC FATHERS

For an adequate understanding of the Apostolic Fathers
we have to deal with them historically—that is to say, in relation to the environment in which, and in relation to which,
they wrote. This environment can be viewed from several
perspectives. First of all, the Apostolic Fathers obviously
lived and wrote within the Christian community. The Church
provides the fundamental environment of their life and
thought. But the Church cannot be viewed as existing in a
vacuum. The Church was closely related to Judaism and to
various Gnostic groups; it was not completely uniform in
organization or in doctrine. Second, the Apostolic Fathers
lived and wrote in the Graeco-Roman world of the late first
century and the early second. They did not suppose that they
were writing timeless theological treatises. They were concerned with the problems to be encountered in the Roman
state and in relation to the various kinds of cultural activity
present in it.

We shall examine first the relation of the state to them and
their relation to it, and later their relation to Judaism, Gnosticism, and Hellenistic culture.

I.   State and Church in the Early Second Century

In determining the historical setting within which the
Apostolic Fathers wrote, we are fortunate enough to possess
two documents which bear directly upon the relation of the

Roman state to the Church. These are letters written by
Pliny the Younger, imperial legate to the province of Bithynia
and Pontus on the Black Sea, to the emperor Trajan, and by
Trajan to Pliny. The exchange of correspondence took place
in the year A.D. 112.

A. Pliny to Trajan

It is my custom, your majesty, to refer everything about
which I have doubts to you; for who can better give guidance
to my hesitation or instruction to my ignorance?

I have never attended investigations of the Christians, and
therefore I do not know what should be investigated or punished, and to what extent it should be done. I was quite uncertain as to whether or not some distinction should be made
on grounds of age, and whether a weak person was no different from stronger people; whether or not pardon should be
granted to one who had completely given up being a Christian; and whether the name itself, if apart from particular
crimes, or the crimes attaching to the name were to be
punished.

Meanwhile I took the following course in dealing with
those who were reported to me as Christians. I asked them if
they were Christians. If they acknowledged it, I asked them
a second and a third time, with the threat of punishment, and
if they persevered I ordered them executed. For I had no
doubt that, whatever they confessed, certainly such stub-
bornness and inflexible obstinacy ought to be punished.
There were others of a similar insanity who were Roman
citizens; I gave orders for them to be sent to the capital.

Presently, because the case was in process, as usually happens the charge spread more widely and more accusations
arrived. An anonymous sheet was sent in, containing the
names of many. As for those who denied that they were or
had been Christians, when after me they invoked the gods
and offered incense and wine to your image—which I had

ordered brought along with the images of the gods for this purpose—and furthermore cursed Christ (those who are really Christians, it is said, cannot be forced to do any of these things), I decided to have them released. Others on the list said that they were Christians but then denied it; they had been, but had stopped, some many years earlier, a few even twenty years past. All of these reverenced the images of you and the gods and cursed Christ.

They asserted that this was the substance of their fault or error: they were accustomed to meet a fixed day before dawn, to say a hymn antiphonally to Christ, as to a god, and bind themselves with an oath—not for performing any crime but not to commit thefts, robberies, or adulteries, nor to break an oath or to refuse to repay a deposit on demand. When this was done they were accustomed to depart, then to meet again for a meal which was ordinary and harmless. They had stopped doing this after my edict in which, in accordance with your orders, I forbade the existence of sodalities. Therefore I considered it all the more necessary to seek for information from two slave women called "deaconesses"—even by torture. I found nothing but a crude and exaggerated superstition. Therefore I suspended proceedings and hastened to consult you.

The matter seemed worthy of consultation, especially because of the number of those affected. For many of all ages and every rank, indeed of both sexes, are endangered and will be endangered. The contagion of this superstition has spread not only through the cities but even to villages and the countryside; but it appears that it can be checked and corrected. Certainly it is clear that temples formerly desolate are coming to be filled, and the sacred rites long abandoned are being taken up again, and there is a trade in fodder for sacrificial animals for which buyers were previously scarce. From this it can easily be inferred that the masses can be reclaimed if there is an opportunity for recanting.

B. Trajan to Pliny

My dear Secundus,

You have taken the proper course in handling the cases of
those who were reported to you as Christians, for nothing
can be established as a universal principle with a fixed form.
They are not to be sought out. If they are accused and
convicted, they must be punished, but in such a way that
anyone who denies that he is a Christian and can prove it
by reverencing our gods, even if he was previously suspect,
may obtain pardon by recanting.

Anonymous accusations, however, must not play a part in
any criminal case. They are characteristic of the worst possible example and are alien to the spirit of our time.

. . . .

The letters are a credit to the enlightened Roman admin-
istrative officials of the second century. Pliny obviously regards Roman religion as closely related to the life of the
Roman state; he cannot understand those who are unwilling
to use religious forms in attesting their loyalty to the state;
all he asks for is compromise. He sees willingness to compromise among some who call themselves Christians, and he is
therefore determined to break the spirit of civil disobedience.
The superstitious nature of Christianity means that right-
thinking men are bound to reject it. Yet while he is anxious
to suppress Christianity, he is not trying to exterminate Christians. He wants to provide every opportunity for recantation.
The emperor shares his attitude. The health and security of
society is the most important matter. Anonymous accusations,
common enough in the reign of Domitian, cannot be accepted; Christians are not to be persecuted, though they
have to be prosecuted. The basic point is that there must
be an opportunity for what the Christians would call
repentance.

C.   Christian Statements

From the Christian side the First Letter of Clement, though written somewhat earlier, reflects an equally conciliatory attitude. Christians pray for guidance "to do what is good and pleasing" before God and before the rulers of the state (60:2).

> Grant that we may be obedient to thy almighty and glorious name and to our rulers and governors upon earth. Thou, Master, hast given the power of sovereignty to them, through thy excellent and inexpressible might, so that we may know the glory and honor given them by thee and be subject to them, in no wise resisting thy will. To them, O Lord, give health, peace, concord, stability, so that they may administer without offense the governance which thou hast given them. For thou, heavenly Master, King of the ages, hast given the sons of men glory and honor and power over what is on earth; do thou, O Lord, direct their will according to what is good and pleasing before thee, so that with piety in peace and gentleness they may administer the power given them by thee, and may find thee propitious (60:4–61:2).

Similarly, Clement is quite willing to use the Roman army, with the emperor at its head, as a model for Christian order (37:1–3); and when he speaks of the martyrs (in the reign of Nero) he ascribes their misfortunes not to the Roman state but to "jealousy"—apparently within the Christian community (5:2–6:2).

The martyr Ignatius himself criticizes his guards as inhuman (Rom. 5:1) but says nothing about the justice of his case or of his judges. Indeed, he is eager to prevent influential Roman Christians from preventing his death (Rom. 4:1). The emphasis he lays upon wild animals as the instrument of his execution keeps him from mentioning human judges or executioners; he thus avoids conflict with the Roman state and its officials. Only occasionally does he mention them, stating that Jesus Christ was nailed (to the cross) under

Pontius Pilate and the tetrarch Herod (Smyrn. 1:2) and that
visible rulers will be judged if they do not believe in the
blood of Christ (6:1).

Polycarp too, well aware of the existence of martyrs (Phil.
9:1), urges his readers to pray for emperors, authorities, and
rulers (12:3; cf. 1 Tim. 2:1-2), though he correlates this
prayer with one for "those who persecute and hate you"
(Matt. 5:44) and for "the enemies of the cross" (Paul, Phil.
3:18).

In the first Similitude of Hermas the opposition between
the Church and the state is much more radically expressed.
The Christian lives temporarily in an alien city, whose ruler
can say to him, "I do not wish you to dwell in this city; go
out from this city because you do not use my laws." In
Hermas' view this sentence is just. "Either use my laws or
go out from my country." In the Roman Empire, then, the
Christian can never be other than a resident alien. In the
second Vision the coming of a great tribulation is predicted;
and in the ninth Similitude we read of those who have suffered for the name of the Son of God and have given up their
lives (9, 28, 2). It is hard, however, to identify any particular
persecution to which Hermas may be referring.

The attitude of Hermas is characteristic of writers of
apocalypses. Generally speaking, they are opposed to existing political structures and predict their imminent collapse.
The contrast between Hermas' attitude and that, for example, of 1 Clement is not accounted for simply on literary
grounds. There are differences of temperament, of theological outlook, and perhaps of circumstances.

Finally, about the year 167, we find the aged Polycarp a
martyr at Smyrna. The attitude of the Roman officials remains conciliatory but firm. First, the captain of police urges
Polycarp to take part in the usual formalities; next, the proconsul of Asia himself tries to persuade Polycarp to take an
oath by the good fortune of Caesar and to say, "Away with
the godless." Polycarp employs the latter formula against his

pagan opponents, and the proconsul has to ask him to curse Christ. All his appeals for recantation meet with no response, and finally he has to burn Polycarp alive. Polycarp recognizes that the proconsul is trying to acquit him and is pretending not to know who he is. Had there been time, he says, he would have discussed the nature of Christianity with him, for Christians have been taught to render suitable honor to powers and authorities appointed by God (Mart. 10:2). The conflict cannot be resolved.

D.   Lucian on Christianity

Apart from the letters of Pliny and Trajan, we possess practically no pagan testimonies to the life of Christians in the early second century. The only texts which may possibly shed some light on it come from the latter years of the century, but since they are describing an earlier situation, we venture to quote them. Both come from essays in which the satirist Lucian is attacking charlatans in Asia Minor—one on the ground that he imposed upon the Christians, the other on the ground that he opposed them. Lucian is no enthusiast for Christianity (or for anything else), but he seems to pay Christians a certain grudging respect.

The first text comes from his work *On the Death of Peregrinus*. This Peregrinus was a wandering Sophist whose career reached a climax when he committed suicide in public in the year 165.

At that time Peregrinus learned the marvelous wisdom of the Christians, since he was in company with their priests and scribes in Palestine. More than that, he readily made them look like children, being a prophet and president and synagogue chief all at once, and all by himself. He interpreted and explained some of their books, but many he composed himself. They thought of him as a god and used him as a legislator and chose him as their leader; but still, strangely enough, they worship the man who was executed in Palestine, since he introduced this new cult to human life.

Then on this account Proteus (Peregrinus) was seized and thrown into prison, an event which procured him no slight renown for the rest of his life, as well as a reputation for miracle-working and the fame which he loved. When he had been imprisoned, the Christians considered the affair a disaster and did everything they could to secure his release. When this proved impossible, other assistance of all sorts was rendered, not sporadically but with zeal. From the earliest dawn old women, widows, and orphan children were to be seen waiting by the prison, and men of rank among them slept with him after bribing the guards. They brought in all sorts of suppers, and their sacred discourses were read, and the most excellent Peregrinus (such was still his name) was considered a new Socrates by them. Some came down even from the cities of Asia, sent by the Christians from their common fund, to help and plead for and encourage the man. They show extraordinary effort whenever such a thing happens which affects their common interest. In short, they spare nothing. And indeed, because of Peregrinus' bonds, many gifts of money were made to him at this time and he made no little profit out of it.

Those wretches have persuaded themselves that they are all going to be immortal and will live forever, so that they despise death and voluntarily give themselves up—most of them. Furthermore, their lawgiver—I mean the first one—persuaded them that they are all brothers, and that when they have once been converted and have denied the Greek gods, they should worship that executed Sophist and live according to his laws. So they despise everything equally and hold everything in common, having accepted such ideas without a rational faith. If any charlatan or humbug who is skillful in such matters came among them, he soon grew rich by imposing on these stupid people.

But Peregrinus was released by the then governor of Syria, a man who enjoyed philosophy and knew his folly and was aware that he would willingly have died in order to acquire fame. . . . A second time he left his country in his wanderings, using the Christians as an adequate source of supplies; they cared for him ungrudgingly in everything.

For some time he was fed thus, but then having offended them in some way—for he was seen, I think, eating food forbidden among them—they no longer helped him and he was reduced to poverty.

The second text is from the *Alexander*, a book about a prophet who won converts to the worship of his sacred snake.

When many intelligent men combined against him, as if they were recovering from deep drunkenness, especially those who were followers of Epicurus . . . he made a proclamation in order to frighten them, saying that Pontus was full of atheists and Christians who ventured to utter the worst blasphemies against him. He ordered men to drive such people away with stones, if they wanted to have the favor of the god (his snake). . . .

[On the first day of Alexander's mysteries] there was a proclamation to this effect: "If any atheist or Christian or Epicurean has come to spy on the rites, let him flee; but let those who believe in the god perform the mysteries with good fortune." Then, right at the beginning, came the expulsion, which he led by saying, "Out with the Christians," and the whole crowd responded, "Out with the Epicureans."

These passages from Lucian contain odd echoes of the religious life of Christians as revealed in the Apostolic Fathers. The description of Peregrinus has often reminded scholars of the picture of Ignatius found in his letters, and it has been suggested that Lucian was parodying the letters themselves, adding further Christian traits from his own observations. The notion that Pontus was full of atheists and Christians may be compared with what Pliny says about Pontus in his letter. And the statement of Alexander at the beginning of his mysteries reminds us of what the Didache says about the Eucharist: "Give not what is holy to the dogs" (9:5), and of the liturgical formula (10:6):

> If anyone is holy, let him come;
> if anyone is not, let him repent.

This is not to claim that Lucian had definite information about points like these. It is simply to say that they illustrate some of the ways in which the writings of the Apostolic Fathers are related to their environment.

II. Judaism and Jewish Christianity

The environment with which we are concerned was by no means uniform or monolithic. There were other significant aspects of life in the Graeco-Roman world with which the Apostolic Fathers were related; and among these the most important were the thought worlds of Judaism and Gnosticism. The relations were both explicit and implicit. We begin with explicit references.

A. Judaism

The most obvious relation to Judaism to be found in the writings of the Apostolic Fathers lies in their common use of the Old Testament. According to Clement, Christ himself through the Holy Spirit speaks in Old Testament texts (22:1). According to Ignatius, "the divine prophets lived according to Christ Jesus" (Magn. 8:2); they were his "disciples in the Spirit" and were raised from the dead by him (9:2). Jesus is the true high priest and the door of the Father, "through which enter Abraham and Isaac and Jacob and the prophets . . ." (Philad. 9). Polycarp does not explicitly quote from the Old Testament but alludes to verses from it. The Didache ascribes verses from the prophet Malachi to "the Lord" (14:3) and quotes from Zechariah (16:7). Barnabas largely is concerned with texts from the Old Testament and with the nature of the covenant. Hermas never quotes from the Old Testament, but it seems to lie behind his whole world view. Finally, Old Testament quotations are fairly common in 2 Clement.

In addition to the Hebrew canon (in Greek translation) most of the Apostolic Fathers make use of what we call the Apocrypha and Pseudepigrapha. Clement knows the books of Wisdom (7:5, 27:5) and Judith (55:4); Ignatius seems to know Wisdom and 4 Maccabees; Polycarp, and perhaps the author of 2 Clement, seems to know Tobit; the Didache contains reflections of Sirach; Barnabas makes use of 2 Baruch, 2 Esdras, and 1 Enoch; and Hermas reflects the form of 2 Esdras.[1] This is to say that these writers come out of an environment in which Jewish piety is significant.

Indeed, in many of their writings there is no criticism of Judaism whatever. Such is the case in 1 Clement and Hermas; and in Polycarp and the Didache criticism is only implicit (in the sense that Christianity is exclusive). In 2 Clement (2:3) we read that Christians "have become many more than those who seemed to have God"—but nothing is made of the point. Ignatius and Barnabas, however, emphasize the differences more strongly. Ignatius argues that Christianity transcends Judaism because in it is found the grace brought by Jesus Christ (Magn. 8–10); he is primarily concerned, however, not with Jews as such but the Judaizers within the Christian community. "It is better to hear Christianity from the circumcised than Judaism from the uncircumcised" (Philad. 6:1). Barnabas is far more radical. He is opposed to the Jewish law—literally understood—the cultus, and the temple; and he states that the covenant does not belong to both Jews and Christians, or first to Jews and then to Christians, but to Christians alone. The odd thing about both Ignatius and Barnabas is that as they write against Judaizers or Jews they make use of materials both Jewish and Jewish-Christian in origin. Evidently there was no clear or absolute break between Church and synagogue.

In addition, the moral teaching of all the Apostolic Fathers is indisputably based upon the teaching current in contemporary Judaism. Though naturally, as in Judaism itself, some Hellenistic motifs are present (especially in 1 Clement and Hermas),[2] the basic tone of the teaching is best paral-

---

[1] Cf. R. Joly, *Hermas: Le Pasteur* (Paris, 1958), 47.
[2] Clement; W. Jaeger, *Early Christianity and Greek Paideia* (Cambridge, Mass., 1961); Hermas: Joly, *op. cit.*, 47-54.

leled in Jewish literature, including the Dead Sea Scrolls.

In recent times it has been urged, especially by J. Danié-lou,[3] that as a group the Apostolic Fathers reflect Jewish Christianity, and that—together with apocryphal writings of the early second century and much early Christian Gnosti-cism—they prove that as a whole early Christianity passed through a period in which this kind of theological thinking was dominant, before the rise of "Hellenistic theology."

In general, it is undeniable that Jewish and Jewish-Chris-tian motifs exist in the writings of the Apostolic Fathers. But certain distinctions must be made. The materials provided in the "two-ways" sections of the Didache (chs. 1–6) and Bar-nabas (chs. 18–20) are almost exclusively Jewish in origin, and the Eucharistic prayers in Didache (chs. 9–10) are based on Jewish thanksgivings. Barnabas seems to rely on Jewish collections of Old Testament passages. Most of what Hermas writes can be paralleled in Jewish documents, including the Dead Sea Scrolls.

On the other hand, the letters of Ignatius reflect a Chris-tianity which is much less close to Judaism, even though at some points his thought seems to be developed out of Jewish-Christian materials. Similarly, Clement, though formally close to Old Testament ideas, treats them in a manner in which Greek and Jewish attitudes are blended. The didacticism of Polycarp has little to do with Judaism.

This is to say that while the "unofficial" documents among the writings of the Apostolic Fathers are representative of Jewish Christianity—the Didache, Barnabas, Hermas—the "official" documents reflect a Christianity which is seeking to express itself in Graeco-Roman terms (see Section IV).

III.   Gnosticism and Magic

Much less direct than any contacts with Judaism are the contacts of the Apostolic Fathers with Gnosticism. This reli-gious movement, which drew upon Jewish, Christian, and

[3] *Théologie du Judéo-Christianisme* (Tournai, 1958).

pagan motifs in its development, was beginning to flourish in the early second century and in all the areas in which Christians were to be found. In Ignatius' time a Samaritan named Menander was teaching that he had been sent down from the highest heaven as Savior for the salvation of men, to rescue them from the power of the angels who were emitted by the First Power's Thought, and made the world. He provided his disciples with magical "knowledge" so that they might overcome the angels, and when the disciples were baptized "into him," they received both resurrection and immortality; they would never die.[4] As I have elsewhere suggested, his interpretation of baptism looks like a distortion of the Pauline teaching about dying and rising with Christ; and what he says about immortality reminds us of Ignatius' statement that the Eucharistic bread is "the drug of immortality, the antidote for dying" (Eph. 20:2). Ignatius, like the Gnostics, is "able to know heavenly things and the angelic locations and the archontic conjunctions" (Trall. 5:2). But we should beware of viewing Ignatius as a Gnostic. The kind of mysterious language he uses is not confined to Gnostic groups. After all, Paul himself—like some of the rabbis— visited "the third heaven" and entered paradise (2 Cor. 12:2-4). Indeed, the section of Ignatius' letter in which he speaks of "heavenly things" is full of reminiscences of Paul's letter.

Another Gnostic teacher, early in the second century, was Saturninus, who we know taught at Antioch. The only point of possible contact between him and Ignatius lies in Saturninus' doctrine that "the Savior is unbegotten, incorporeal, and without form" and "appeared as a man in semblance."[5] To this idea Ignatius was resolutely opposed. Jesus Christ was both "begotten and unbegotten"; he was God incarnate (Eph. 7:2). Only godless unbelievers teach that his suffering was only in semblance (Trall. 10). Unfortunately, Ignatius did

[4] Irenaeus, *Adv. haer.* 1, 23, 5.
[5] *Ibid.*, 1, 24, 1.

not regard it as right to record their names (Smyrn. 5:3); otherwise we might have encountered Saturninus' name.

It is conceivable that at one point 2 Clement 12:2 provides a quotation from the semi-Gnostic Gospel of the Egyptians, although he may be relying on oral tradition: "When the Lord himself was asked by someone when his kingdom would come, he said, 'When the two are one and the outside as the inside and the male with the female neither male nor female.'" But he provides exegesis which is quite unGnostic. "The two are one" when we speak with one another in truth; the outside is the body, the inside the soul; "neither male nor female" implies the absence of sexual desire.

Polycarp may be attacking the doctrines of the dualist Marcion in the seventh chapter of his letter, though his remarks seem rather general.

> Everyone who does not confess that Jesus Christ has come in the flesh is an anti-Christ (1 John 4:2-3; 2 John 7); and whoever does not confess the testimony of the cross is of the devil; and whoever perverts the oracles of the Lord for his own lusts, and says that there is neither resurrection nor judgment—this man is the first-born of Satan.

Irenaeus tells us that Polycarp called Marcion "the first-born of Satan,"[6] but presumably he could have used the phrase against other Gnostics.

Finally, Hermas seems to have attacked Gnostic doctrines. In Sim. 9, 22 he criticizes those who lay false claims to knowledge, and in Sim. 5, 7, 2 he opposes those who say that the flesh is perishable and that therefore sins of the flesh have no importance. Such men may advise against repentance (Sim. 8, 6, 5). But Hermas can hardly have found Gnosticism a matter of cardinal importance.[7]

It should be added that there is not the slightest trace of

---

[6] *Ibid.*, 3, 3, 4.

[7] M. Dibelius (*Der Hirt des Hermas* [Tübingen, 1923], 630) insists that he knew Gnostics.

Gnostic controversy or influence in 1 Clement, the Didache, or Barnabas. Perhaps this silence indicates that Gnosticism was not a problem in the first century (1 Clement, Didache) or, in the second, in the area where Barnabas was written. If the author of 2 Clement was really using the Gospel of the Egyptians, it is clear that he did not recognize it as Gnostic.

The opponents, or some of the opponents, of Ignatius, Polycarp, and Hermas, on the other hand, seem to be fairly close to Gnosticism—not to the authors of the great Gnostic systems which flourished in Hadrian's reign (117–138) and later, but to the "garden variety" Gnosticism fairly widespread a little earlier.

Another feature of the religious background of the Apostolic Fathers which deserves mention is *magic*, closely related to Gnosticism and, like it, promising control over an environment largely hostile. It is mentioned twice in the Didache. The first time it occurs in an expansion of the commandments not to commit adultery or to steal; the additional commandments not to use magic or spells are appropriate in this context (2:2). In the second instance, magic and spells are mentioned as characteristic of "the way of death," and again they follow "adulteries, lusts, fornications, and thefts" (5:1). Similarly, spells and magic are part of "the way of the Black One" in Barnabas (20:1).

According to Ignatius (Eph. 19:3) the appearance of a new star at the birth of Christ brought about what he calls the dissolution of magic and the disappearance of every bond of wickedness. Presumably what he has in mind is that the astral powers often invoked by magicians were thrown into disorder, thus becoming no longer accessible to them. From the earliest times Christians, like the Old Testament writers, were hostile to magic and magicians; this point is made clear in the stories in Acts about Simon Magus (8:9-11), Bar Jesus-Elymas (13:6-12) and the books worth 50,000 denarii burned at Ephesus (19:19).

IV. Hellenistic Culture

Finally we come to the elusive relationship between the Apostolic Fathers and the culture, largely literary, of their time. This culture is most conspicuously reflected in the First Letter of Clement, but it is also present in the letters of Ignatius and in the Shepherd of Hermas.

A. Clement

Clement's letter begins with a vividly rhetorical description of the ideal state of the Corinthian church and its past glories; the Corinthians were "adorned with most virtuous and honorable citizenship" (2:8). When he turns from past to present, his style comes closer to that of the Greek Old Testament, and finally he quotes the story of Cain and Abel from it. They provide the prime examples of the result of jealousy, to which he ascribes the Corinthian troubles. Then he adds six more examples, all of them carefully stylized: "because of jealousy," "jealousy made," "jealousy forced," "because of jealousy," "jealousy brought down," "because of jealousy." A rhetorician's model sentence follows:

> But, to cease from the ancient examples, let us come to those athletes who lived in the times nearest us; let us take the noble examples of our own generation (5:1).

These examples are Peter and Paul, whose sufferings were due to jealousy. To them Clement adds "a great multitude of the elect," especially Christian women who were persecuted as "Danaids and Dircae" (6:2)—presumably because they were forced to take part in spectacles in which like the daughters of Danaus they were given as prizes in athletic contests and like Dirce were dragged to death by a wild bull.[8] He concludes with two generalizations about jealousy:

[8] For martyrdoms of this sort see Tacitus, *Ann.* 15, 44, 7; for the realism of Nero's mythological plays see Suetonius, *Nero* 11, 2; 12, 2.

it "has estranged wives from husbands" and along with strife has "overthrown great cities and uprooted great nations" (6:3-4).

Clement is quite fond of using examples to prove a general statement. "Let us review all the generations," he writes, "and let us learn that in generation after generation the Master has given a place of repentance to those who will turn to him" (7:5). As examples, he provides the cases of Noah and Jonah before turning to quotations from the prophets. A little later we find examples of faithful obedience —Enoch, Noah, and Abraham—and the last of these becomes the first of a new collection which illustrates "faith and hospitality"; it continues with Lot and Rahab. Obviously the form, like the content, of these compilations is not strictly Greek. Clement has Jewish models in Sirach and the Wisdom of Solomon (the mention of the "place of repentance" in the quotation above comes from Wisdom 12:10) and a Christian model in the Epistle to the Hebrews, which he knows. But he is working on the border line between cultures, as another instance clearly shows. In chapter 55 he appeals to the leader of the revolt to accept voluntary exile (a theme often used among contemporary rhetoricians) and backs it up with examples.

> Let us also bring forward examples from the gentiles. Many kings and rulers, when a time of pestilence has set in, have followed the counsel of oracles and have given themselves up to death so that they might deliver their subjects through their own blood. Many have gone away from their own cities so that there might not be further sedition.

Only after this section on paganism does Clement turn to Christian examples and to the cases of Judith and Esther (ch. 55).

There are three other passages in which Clement's use of Hellenistic sources is abundantly clear. In chapter 37 he

evidently uses Paul's picture of the Church as analogous to
a human body (1 Cor. 12—itself Graeco-Roman in origin
and ethos) as a point of departure for his own comparison
of the Church to the Roman army, with emperor, generals,
prefects, tribunes, centurions, and lieutenants. In chapters
25 and 26 he discusses the death and "resurrection" of the
Arabian phoenix as used by God to show "the greatness of
his promise." And in chapter 20 he takes as a model the peace
and harmony of the universe.

This discussion of cosmic order has led to considerable
controversy. Forty years ago the Abbé Bardy drew attention
to the Stoic parallels to the chapter and suggested that
Clement was following a written source of Stoic origin.[9]
Twenty years later, L. Sanders did little more than to complete the proof that the theme of cosmic harmony was popular in Clement's day among Greek writers.[10] In 1950, W. C.
van Unnik pointed out that the theme is also to be found in
Jewish literature and may have reached Clement via Judaism.[11] The Greek origin of Clement's picture was upheld
again in an article by W. Jaeger; he suggested that the themes
of the earth being pregnant or fruitful (20:4; cf. Philo, *Opif.*
43) and the springs offering their breasts for the life of men
(20:10, cf. Philo, *Opif.* 133) were derived from Greek poetic
sources, not from Philo or other Jewish writers.[12] Jaeger's
results were rather conjectural, and a better proof is provided
by J. J. Thierry: the reference to the harmonious intercourse
of "the smallest animals" (20:10), like the sentence preceding
it, is very close to Cicero's discussion of providence and its
operations (*De natura deorum* 2, 120–123) and therefore presumably comes from a Greek philosophical source.[13]

Further attempts, like Jaeger's, to prove Clement's ac-

[9] *Recherches de science religieuse* 13 (1922), 73-85.

[10] *L'hellénisme de saint Clément de Rome et le paulinisme* (Louvain, 1943).

[11] *Vigiliae Christianae* 4 (1950), 181-189.

[12] *Rheinisches Museum* 102 (1959), 330-340.

[13] *Vigiliae Christianae* 14, (1960), 235-244.

quaintance with Greek poetry are not especially convincing in detail,[14] but at any rate they prove that he was conversant with the kind of language poets used. Similarly, the effort of C. Eggenberger to show that Clement made use of the writings of Dio Chrysostom (early second century) was not a success;[15] but he did demonstrate—as Sanders had already done—that the themes utilized by the two authors were much the same.

One cannot maintain that Clement was simply a Hellenist. When he lists army officers in chapter 37 he includes what we translated as "lieutenants." Actually the rank in question is that of a "captain of fifty" (*pentēkontarchos*), which occurs not in the Roman army but in the Old Testament—and in the Dead Sea Scrolls! We therefore see that he mixes Greek and Jewish ideas; he lives on the borderline between cultures, insofar as we can differentiate the two in his time and in his place.[16]

B. Ignatius and Polycarp

What has been written by theologians on the style and the Hellenism of Ignatius is largely unhistorical. There are only two studies of his relation to Graeco-Roman thought or, indeed, to any thought but his own. The first, by Otto Perler, proves that he was deeply influenced by the Hellenistic Jewish homily known as 4 Maccabees and that his style, like that of this work, must be classified as belonging to the florid Asianism of his time.[17] The second, by H. Riesenfeld, builds on Perler's foundation and mentions Ignatius' closeness to Melito of Sardis and his use of examples presumably derived

[14] A. W. Ziegler, *Neue Studien zum ersten Klemensbrief* (München, 1958).

[15] *Die Quellen der politischen Ethik des 1. Klemensbriefes* (Zurich, 1951).

[16] Cf. Exod. 18:21, 25; 1 Macc. 3:55; Dead Sea War Scroll, col. III, line 17; Y. Yadin, *The Scroll of the War of the Sons of Light against the Sons of Darkness* (Oxford, 1962), 59. For further Greek elements in this passage cf. W. Jaeger, *Early Christianity and Greek Paideia* (Cambridge, Mass., 1961), 19-20.

[17] *Rivista di archeologia cristiana* 25 (1949), 47-72.

from his training in rhetoric—medical (Eph. 7:2, 10:2; Polyc. 2:1); musical (Eph. 4:1-2; Philad. 1:2); nautical (Polyc. 2:3.); and athletic (Polyc. 1:3, 2:3, 3:1).[18]

I have elsewhere suggested that Ignatius' acquaintance with Judaism is indirect and that he viewed Jewish Christianity without enthusiasm. When we combine with this notion the observation that he made use of Graeco-Roman rhetoric, we certainly find him to be a representative of the coming Hellenized Church.

On the other hand, Polycarp's letter is nothing but a patchwork of earlier Christian sources. It cannot be described as Jewish or Greek; Polycarp does not reflect any definite cultural attitude, though with 2 Clement (9:1) he attacks those who deny the doctrines, originally Jewish, of resurrection and judgment (7:1).

C. Writers Reflecting Jewish Christianity

Some writers among the Apóstolic Fathers show practically no acquaintance with Hellenistic or Graeco-Roman ways of thinking. Such is the case with Polycarp, as we have just seen; it is also the case in the Didache, in Barnabas, and in 2 Clement (except for an athletic metaphor developed in ch. 7).

In the Shepherd of Hermas, however, as R. Joly has argued,[19] there is a definite relationship to the Hellenistic romance and to Hellenistic piety, though not—as Reitzenstein and Dibelius supposed—to the Hellenistic writings. The most striking resemblance between Hermas and any Greek literary document is to be found by considering the Pinax of Cebes, a syncretistic ethical treatise in which virtues and vices are personified much as they are in the Shepherd. As Joly readily admits, Hermas' ideas are his own; but he expresses them in a way reminiscent of the Pinax. It is a matter of what A. D. Nock called "external Hellenization."

[18] Texte und Untersuchungen 79 (1961), 312-322.
[19] Hermas: Le Pasteur (Paris, 1958), 47-57.

Finally, it is undeniable that the fragments we possess from Papias' Exegeses of the Dominical Oracles reveal him as a Christian close to the Judaism of his time, partly because of his enthusiasm for oral tradition but more notably because of his millenarian views. There are two points, however, at which Greek ways of thinking seem to be reflected—in addition to the obvious fact that his book was written in Greek. First, his discussion of oral tradition in the preface to his book betrays considerable care for a well-balanced sentence; and his criticism of rhetoric ("not like the many did I take pleasure in those who spoke the most") is not unrhetorical, any more than is his mention of a "living and surviving voice." Second, whether Papias or his informant, the elder, is ultimately responsible for the defense of Mark provided in the Exegeses, the defense seems to show some knowledge of what a literary critic might expect to find in a book. The Gospel of Mark has the virtues of truth and of relative completeness; it does not possess literary order.[20]

[20] For a more complete analysis see *The Earliest Lives of Jesus* (New York, 1961), 14-19.

Chapter V

THE THEOLOGY OF THE APOSTOLIC
FATHERS

There are two ways in which the theology of the Apostolic Fathers can be discussed. One is by treating them more or less as a group and by laying emphasis on their common teaching. This approach has the advantage of drawing attention to their common Christian faith, but it tends to minimize their individuality and the differences in approach which exist among them. The other way is, of course, to treat them as individuals, while bearing in mind that they were not speaking for themselves alone but for the communities out of which, and to which, they were writing.

We shall endeavor to gain some of the advantages of both modes of discussion, by first mentioning some of the common characteristics of their thought and then dealing with them as individual writers. This method may result in doing less than justice to some among them, but it will give greater credit to the creative originality of the most important theologian among them, Ignatius of Antioch.

I. Some Common Elements

Chief among the common elements in the Apostolic Fathers is their doctrine of God as creator, providential ruler, redeemer, and judge. This doctrine, derived from the Old Testament and the apostolic writings as well as from the worship of the Christian community, is so frequently expressed or implied that we do not need to give examples at this point.

More striking is the selection of titles which the Apostolic
Fathers use in relation to Jesus Christ. "One of the characteristic traits of the Jewish Christian theology," writes Père
Daniélou, "is the great diversity of the expressions it uses in
speaking of the Son of God." He points out that within the
New Testament itself there are forty-three titles or names
applied to Jesus, though not all of these were used by Christians in post-Apostolic times.[1] Indeed, when we look at the
writings of the Apostolic Fathers, we encounter a distinct
narrowing of this variety, not so much in 1 Clement or Ignatius but more notably in the Didache, Barnabas, and Hermas.

For example, the title "Son of Man," frequently employed
in the Gospels (though outside them only once, in Acts 7:56),
occurs only twice in the Apostolic Fathers. Ignatius speaks
of Jesus as human and divine, "Son of man and Son of God"
(Eph. 20:2) Barnabas cites Old Testament verses in which
Jesus is "not son of man but Son of God" (12:10-11). The
Johannine expression "Lamb of God" occurs nowhere, though
both Clement (16:7) and Barnabas (5:2) refer to Jesus the
words of Isaiah (53:7) in which the Suffering Servant is
likened to a lamb. The title "Wisdom," sometimes applied to
Jesus in the New Testament, and by later writers to the Holy
Spirit, is never applied to him by the Apostolic Fathers,
though Clement (chs. 57–58) personifies the Wisdom who
spoke in the book of Proverbs.

Another title, found only in sermons and prayers in the
book of Acts (3:13, 26; 4:27, 30), recurs only in prayers in
the writings of the Apostolic Fathers: this is the title "child,"
used of Jesus. In the prayer of 1 Clement, Jesus Christ the
beloved child of God is the one through whom the elect have
been called from darkness to light (59:2-3); ultimately all
nations will know that he is God's child (59:4). The emphasis
falls upon election and also upon the revelation given through
him. In the prayers of the Didache we learn that God's child
Jesus was the one through whom the vine of David, life,

[1] J. Daniélou, *Théologie du Judéo-Christianisme* (Tournai, 1958), 199.

knowledge, faith, and immortality were made known (9:2-3; 10:2); he was the one through whom God blessed Christians with spiritual food and drink and eternal life (10:3). He was primarily the instrument of revelation. Finally, in the prayer in the Martyrdom of Polycarp, "the beloved and blessed child Jesus Christ" is the one "through whom we have received knowledge of thee" (14:2), and Polycarp glorifies God through Jesus Christ, who is not only high priest but also beloved child of God (14:3). A doxology at the end of the Martyrdom (20:2) is addressed to God through his only-begotten child Jesus Christ.

The title used in Polycarp's prayer, that of high priest, occurs within the New Testament in the epistle to the Hebrews and is taken over from Hebrews by Clement, who speaks of Jesus Christ as "the high priest of our offerings" and "the high priest and guardian of our souls" (36:1, 61:3; ch. 64). Both Ignatius and Polycarp use the title in their letters. Ignatius says that Jesus is the high priest entrusted with the Holy of Holies and with the secret things of God (Philad. 9:1); Polycarp asks that God and the eternal high priest Jesus Christ may edify the community (Phil. 12:2).

In the Apostolic Fathers, as already in Paul, the title "Christ" has become a proper name; and in their writings we frequently encounter such traditional titles as "Son," "Son of God," and "Lord." What makes their writings distinctive, from a Christological point of view, is the special kind of terms they employ, some reflecting Jewish Christianity, others an environment closer to the Hellenistic world in general.

Another title is that which designates Christ as the "name" of God. Daniélou has discussed this term in considerable detail, and he finds it not only in Jewish and Gnostic writings but also in 1 Clement and Hermas.[2] J. Ponthot, on the other hand, has studied the use of it in 1 Clement and the Didache and denies that it refers to Christ directly; "the divine name is an expression of the presence or the action of God," now

[2] *Ibid.*, 199-216.

accessible primarily by means of the work of the Messiah.[3]
According to Hermas (Sim. 9, 14, 5) "the name of the Son
of God is great and incomprehensible, and supports the whole
world" and "the whole creation is supported by the Son of
God." This does not mean, however, that the name is the Son.
It means that "name" is an expression of the presence and
action of the Son.

In addition to doctrines of God and Christ, the Apostolic
Fathers share fairly consistent attitudes toward eschatology,
and to this subject we turn.

In 1 Clement there is very little explicit eschatological
doctrine, for the letter is a practical one, devoting its attention primarily to the present and to the past as affording
warnings or models. Clement does speak of future rewards,
however (e.g., chs. 34–35), and says that the truly religious
will be made manifest "at the visitation of the kingdom of
Christ" (50:3). When he reminds the Corinthians of the
future resurrection, he uses "proofs" not unlike the examples
provided in Paul's letter to the same community (1 Cor. 15).
First he refers to the resurrection of the Lord Jesus Christ
as the "first fruits" (24:1; 1 Cor. 15:20). Then he speaks of
the "resurrections" of day and night and of crops from seeds;
after that he turns to the "paradoxical sign" provided by the
story of the phoenix; and he concludes by giving very free
quotations from the Old Testament, perhaps making use of
an anthology.

In 2 Clement, on the other hand, there is a persistent
eschatological emphasis. Jesus Christ is the judge of living
and dead (1:1); those who do his will are to obtain rest in
the future kingdom and in eternal life (5:5), while others
will receive eternal punishment (6:7), with terrible torture
in unquenchable fire (17:7). It is this present flesh which is
judged and will rise again (9:1). Only repentance and purity
can save it (ch. 8).

Eschatological notes in the Didache are confined to the

[3] *Ephemerides Theologicae Lovanienses* 35 (1959), 339-361.

liturgical section (chs. 7–10) and to the apocalyptic epilogue (ch. 16). The Christian not only prays "thy kingdom come" (8:2) but also asks that the Church may be gathered together into God's kingdom (9:4, 10:5). He prays for grace to come and for this world to pass away; he prays "Marana tha" ("our Lord, come," 10:6). Fiery trials will take place, but then there will be signs in heaven and the resurrection of the righteous dead, and the coming of the Lord on the clouds of heaven (ch. 16). Though the eschatology does not seem to be integrated with the moral imperatives of the Didache, it is obviously important.

The role of eschatology is rather ambiguous in the Shepherd of Hermas. Clearly enough, Hermas thinks in eschatological terms. He announces the forgiveness of sins committed "up to this day," mentions "the last day," and speaks of "the great tribulation which is coming" (Vis. 2, 2, 4-7). For the elect there will be eternal life in the age to come (Vis. 4, 3, 5); it can be compared to summertime; but for others it will be winter, though they will be burned (Sim. 4, 1, 2; 4, 4, 4). The master will come (Sim. 5, 5, 3), though the Son of God has (already?) been made manifest "at the end of the days of the Consummation" (9, 12, 3). The present period is that in which the Church is being built, and the traditional sayings about entering the kingdom of God are referred to entering the Church. Hermas calls upon unworthy ministers to repent before the Church is completed (9, 26, 6). True believers already have a place with the angels—if they continue serving the Lord until the end (9, 27, 3).

These statements are relatively clear, but one wonders how literally they should be taken. Far more important, it would appear, is the constantly reiterated formula, "live to God." As Barberet has pointed out, it resembles what Paul says in Romans 6:10-11 and Galatians 2:19; it means "living in relation to God";[4] and such a life is not explicitly or peculiarly eschatological in nature. The Ninth Similitude, indeed, states

[4] *Recherches de science religieuse* 46 (1958), 397-407.

that the building of the Church has been interrupted so that men may repent (9, 14, 2)—and this statement is repeated at the very end of the book (10, 4).[5]

Similarly, in the Epistle of Barnabas there is a good deal of eschatological language. Barnabas speaks of the present evil age, though the last days are already present (2:1, 4:9, etc.). There will be a future judgment and a time when men will rule over beasts, fish, and birds (4:12, 6:18-19). Barnabas even says that "the day is at hand when all things shall perish with the evil one; 'the Lord and his reward is at hand' (Isa. 40:10)" (21:3). But this language is emptied of any real meaning by the clear statement that "the Lord will make an end of everything in six thousand years" (15:4). At that time the Son will come and "will destroy the time of the wicked one and will judge the godless and will change the sun and the moon and the stars . . ." (15:5). If Barnabas' readers were as intelligent as he says they were, they could not have failed to realize that according to Jewish chronology the world was no more than 5,500 years old, and the end was therefore not very close.

Barnabas relies on the six days of creation, treated as equivalent to a thousand years apiece (cf. 2 Peter 3:8), in reaching his chronological conclusion. Obviously his purpose is to postpone the end for as long as he can.[6]

Among the writings with which we have thus far dealt—largely representatives of Jewish Christianity—only 2 Clement and the Didache clearly present strong eschatological concerns. It is not a question of the date of the writings, for the Didache seems to be relatively early, 2 Clement relatively late. And when we turn to the least Jewish of the Apostolic Fathers, we find a relatively vigorous expression of eschatological thought. This point suggests that simple classi-

---

[5] Cf. 2 Peter 3:9 (Joly).
[6] Cf. A. Hermans in *Ephemerides Theologicae Lovanienses* 35 (1959), 849-876.

fications have, or should have, no place in the early history of Christian doctrine.

Ignatius devotes rather less space to eschatology than do most of the New Testament writers, and it has often been supposed that the subject means little to him. In some measure this supposition is correct; one who is on his way to martyrdom is not likely to concentrate his attention upon the last judgment or the immediate return of Christ. These themes, however, are present in his letters. In Ephesians 11:1 he states that these are the "last times" and urges his readers to fear God's patience so that it may not turn into condemnation. "We should either fear the wrath to come or love the grace which is present—one of the two; only let us be found in Christ Jesus for true life." His use of the name "Christ Jesus" suggests that he has Pauline ideas in mind (see page 167). He continues with the prayer that at the future resurrection he may "be found in the lot of the Ephesian Christians." Obviously, at least here, eschatological ideas are important to him. Similarly, in Ephesians 14:2 he insists upon perseverance; what counts is the power of faith if a man be found (in it) at the end. There is a kingdom of God, still to be inherited (Eph. 16:3; Philad. 3:3), and Jesus Christ is "our common hope" (six times). The Father will raise up those who believe in Christ Jesus (Trall. 9:2—a Pauline idea).[7] There is an end for everything, and a choice between death and life; each man is to go to "his own place" (Magn. 5:1).

To be sure, this eschatology has been realized in part. The incarnation resulted in a new situation, for "all magic was dissolved and every bond of wickedness disappeared; ignorance was abolished and the old kingdom was destroyed" (Eph. 19:3). But something remains to be done. In the unity of Christian worship the powers of Satan are destroyed; in peace every war in heaven and earth is abolished (Eph. 13).

[7] See Bauer 238 *ad loc.*

There is a future judgment for heavenly, as for earthly,
beings if they do not believe in the blood of Christ (Smyrn.
6:1) or, in other words, in the reality of Christ's suffering.
And while Ignatius does speak of fire in relation to his own
impending martyrdom (Rom. 5:3; Smyrn. 4:2), he also says
of those who teach falsely and do not inherit the kingdom
that they, like their hearers, will go to "the unquenchable
fire" (Eph. 16:2; cf. 2 Clem. 17:7).

II.   The Individual Fathers

A.   1 Clement

The doctrine of God expressed in 1 Clement is essentially
the doctrine to be found in Hellenistic Judaism or, more
accurately stated, among Hellenistic Jews. God is "the Father
and Creator of the whole universe" (19:2), the "demiurge
and Master of all" (20:11), to whom the orderliness of everything is due. He is the Father, merciful in every respect and
beneficent (23:1); he exercises providence (24:5). Nothing
is impossible for him except to lie (27:2; perhaps based on
Heb. 6:18).

One title of God, "Most High," has sometimes suggested
that Clement was influenced by paganism or by syncretistic
forms of Judaism. The five examples of it in his letter, however, are all derived from the Greek Old Testament.[8]

By the word of his majesty he established everything
(27:4), and he sees and hears everything (28:1). He rejoices
in his works (33:2). He is all holy, and he gives men "life in
immortality, splendor in righteousness, truth in boldness,
faith in confidence, continence in holiness" (35:1-2). He
needs nothing; he asks for nothing, except for confession to
himself (52:1).

In accordance with Jewish tradition, Clement frequently
refers to God's name and its glorification (43:6), to worship

---

[8] 1 Clem. 29:2 (Deut. 32:8); 45:7 (twice; Dan. 3:26); 52:3 (Ps. 50:14);
59:3 (Is. 57:15).

of it (45:7) as contrasted with bringing blasphemy upon it (47:7). He urges Christians to obey God's all-holy and glorious name and to "tabernacle" with confidence on the most sacred Name of his majesty (58:1, partly an allusion to Prov. 1:23-33, quoted in 57:3-7). God's name is the source of all creation (59:3); it is made known to Christians through Jesus Christ (59:2); it is to be obeyed (60:4). Christians are called by this name, and pray to be pleasing to it (64:1).

God is God alone, but Jesus Christ is his child (59:4), and the scepter of his greatness (16:2). Clement can express an oath thus: "As God lives and as the Lord Jesus Christ lives and as the Holy Spirit . . ." (58:2). Perhaps the most meaningful title of Jesus is "high priest" (36:1, 61:3, 64), a title based on the Epistle to the Hebrews. The origin of the title is obvious when one considers the importance Clement attaches to the blood of Jesus. This blood, precious to his Father, was poured out for men's salvation and brought the grace of repentance to the whole world (7:4). The scarlet thread put out by Rahab symbolized the future redemption of believers through the Lord's blood (12:7), which was given for Christians (21:6). In love Jesus Christ gave his blood for us, his flesh for our flesh, his soul for our souls (49:6). His self-sacrifice was obviously unique, though analogies to it can be provided from kings and rulers among the gentiles who have rescued their subjects through their own blood (55:1). This emphasis too comes from Hebrews, though it, of course, is also Pauline.[9] We shall encounter it again in Ignatius.[10]

The work of the Holy Spirit is presented in a clear fashion. Primarily Clement is concerned with revelation and inspiration when he speaks of the Spirit, the instrument of God in the Old Testament (8:1, 13:1, 16:2, 22:1, 45:2), among the apostles (42:3-4), and for Clement himself (63:2). The Holy

[9] F. Grandchamp, "La doctrine du sang du Christ dans les épîtres de saint Paul," Revue de theologie et de philosophie 11 (1961), 262-271.
[10] The resurrection seems much less important, though it gave assurance to the apostles (42:3); the future resurrection has to be demonstrated (ch. 24).

Spirit was abundantly poured out on the church of Corinth
(2:2). In other words, as Clement says in imitation of Ephesians 4:4-6, for Christians there is one God, one Christ, and
one Spirit of grace poured out upon them (46:6; cf. 58:2,
already mentioned).

Like most of the Apostolic Fathers, Clement never mentions demons or demoniacs. Angels, however, occur in two
quotations from Hebrews (36:2-3) and one from Deuteronomy (29:2), as well as in an explicit reference to "the whole
multitude of his angels . . . ready to serve his will" (34:5).
The primary function of these angels is described in terms
derived from Daniel 7:10 and Isaiah 6:3: "Ten thousand
times ten thousand stood by him, and thousand thousands
served him, and they cried, 'Holy, holy, holy, Lord of Saba-
oth; the whole creation is full of his glory' " (34:6).[11]

Like the angels, men serve and glorify the name of God,
Through Christ, God "called us from darkness to light, from
ignorance to the knowledge of his glorious name" (59:2).
The name of God is mentioned in the last and most specific
part of the letter, and it usually evokes a doxology. By insisting upon order in the old Israel, Moses glorified the name
of the true and only God (43:6, doxology). Persecutors do
not know that the Most High is the defender and protector
of those who with a pure conscience serve his most excellent
name (45:7, doxology). The schismatic Corinthians are
bringing blasphemy upon the name of the Lord (47:7).
Toward the end of the letter, Clement urges his readers to
be obedient to God's all-holy and glorious name and to have
confidence in the most sacred name of his greatness (58:1,
doxology). In the prayer Clement asks for the power to set
his hope on God's creative name (59:3) and to be obedient
to his almighty and glorious name (60:4). Christians are

[11] W. C. van Unnik has shown (*Vigiliae Christianae* 5 [1951], 204-248)
that this passage does not prove that the Sanctus was a part of the early
liturgy.

"called after" his glorious and holy name (64, doxology). This emphasis upon God's name as equivalent to his person in action is, as Quispel, Daniélou, and others have pointed out, Jewish in origin and environment. We encounter the revelation of the name in John 17 and in the prayer of Didache 10:2-3. The relation between tabernacling and the name, expressed in 1 Clement 58:1, is also found in Didache 10:2 and in two Old Testament prophets (Jer. 7:12; Ezek. 43:7).

Such themes, to which more could easily be added, show us that the spiritual environment of Clement, like that of much of the New Testament, is to be found at a point where Jewish and Hellenistic ideas overlap. Clement is neither strictly Jewish nor strictly Greek. He is a Christian who is making use of motifs derived from both thought worlds— insofar as the two thought worlds can really be differentiated.

It is significant that in spite of Clement's strong emphasis upon obeying God by performing the works which he requires, he can state that "we who by his will have been called in Christ Jesus are not made righteous of ourselves or through our wisdom or understanding (1 Cor. 1:19) or piety or the deeds which we have done in holiness of heart, but through the faith by which God Almighty has justified all men from the beginning." But then this faith is not opposed to right actions: "What then shall we do, brothers? Shall we become idle in regard to well-doing, and abandon love?" (32:4– 33:1).

Knopf sadly states that what Clement has done is to combine the Pauline doctrine of justification by faith along with a bad doctrine of synergism (as in James 2:22, Ephesians 2:10, and the Pastoral Epistles). Such a mixture leads on toward the ancient Catholic Church.[12] One might suppose that the advocacy of works of love could be found in the

[12] R. Knopf, *Lehre der zwölf Apostel. Zwei Clemensbriefe* (Tübingen, 1920), 98.

major Pauline epistles; and Knopf's implicit assumption that authentic Christianity is not Catholic demands a certain measure of questioning.

B. 2 Clement

Through Christ men know his Father, the "Father of truth" (3:1, 20:5). Here we find an appellation of God that was fairly common among Christian Gnostics. It occurs in the Gospel of Truth (p. 16, 33); four times in a Valentinian document preserved by Epiphanius (*Pan.* 31, 5, 5.7; 6, 1.4); among the Marcosians (Irenaeus, *Adv. haer.* 1, 15, 2; 20, 2-3); and in the fragments of Heracleon (Origen, *Ioh. comm.* 13, 16). Is it Gnostic? Does its use make 2 Clement a Gnostic book?

The answer to these questions is no. First, Origen himself could use the appellation in his treatise *De principiis* (2, 6, 1). Second, 2 Clement also uses the expression "God of truth" (19:1), which occurs in 1 Esdras 4:40. The spiritual environment of 2 Clement is essentially Jewish, even rabbinic, not Gnostic. God is "the one invisible God, the Father of truth, who sent forth to us the Savior and prince of imperishability, through whom he also revealed to us the truth and the life of heaven" (20:5). He is the "living God" (20:2), who will bring in his kingdom and the last judgment—as the whole sermon shows.

Christ and the Church are closely related in Clement's thought. "Christ the Lord who saved us, though at first he was Spirit, became flesh and thus called us" (9:5). Similarly, the Church—the "first" or primal one—was spiritual, created before the sun and the moon; but she was made manifest in the last days in order to save us; she was made manifest in the flesh of Christ (14:1-3). The author seems to be developing his thought partly as biblical exegesis. Thus he says that "the living Church is the body of Christ," perhaps because of Ephesians 5:23; and he goes on at once to quote Genesis 1:27, also quoted in Ephesians 5:32. "God made man male and female"; the male, he says, is Christ; the female is the Church. (But then how was the Church created before sun and moon?) The subsequent notions about the flesh being the Church and the Spirit being Christ (14:4) simply compound confusion.[13]

C. Ignatius

The theological outlook of Ignatius was strongly influenced by Paul, to whose letters he very frequently alludes, and by John, either as a teacher or as the author of a Gospel. For him God is above Father, and by "Father" he means primarily that God is the Father of Jesus Christ. "There is one God, who manifested himself through Jesus Christ his Son, who is his Word who came forth from silence" (Magn. 8:2). This God, the Most High Father (Rom. inscr.), is merciful (Trall. 12:3) and long-suffering (Eph. 11:1). He is characterized by unity (Eph. 14:1; Trall. 11:2, etc.), by harmony (Magn. 6:1), and by grace (Rom. inscr.). He knows men's secrets (Magn. 3:2) and inspires men's thoughts (Trall. 5:1). We need add no further examples to these; for Ignatius, God is the God revealed in the Old Testament and in the Gospel— as Son, Father, and Spirit (Magn. 13:1).

Like both Paul and John, Ignatius has much more to say about the Son than about the Father. We begin our discussion of his doctrine of Christ with the credal or semi-credal passages in which he sets forth the common faith. The most significant of these are as follows:

1. Our God, Jesus the Christ, was born of Mary, in accordance with the divine plan, of the seed of David and of the Holy Spirit; he was born and was baptized in order by his passion to cleanse the water (Eph. 18:2).
2. Jesus Christ, of the family of David, of Mary, who was truly born, ate and drank, was truly persecuted under Pontius Pilate, was truly crucified and died, in the pres-

[13] On this passage see G. Krüger, "Zu II. Klem. 14, 2," *Zeitschrift für die neutestamentliche Wissenschaft* 31 (1932), 204-205.

> ence of beings in heaven and on earth and under the
> earth, who was truly raised from the dead when his
> Father raised him; in like fashion the Father will also
> raise us who believe in him (Trall. 9).
>
> 3. Our Lord, truly of the family of David after the flesh, Son
>   of God after the will and power of God, truly born of a
>   virgin, baptized by John so that all righteousness might
>   be fulfilled by him, truly nailed in the flesh for us under
>   Pontius Pilate and the tetrarch Herod . . . (Smyrn. 1:1-2).

It is quite evident that whether or not these affirmations are
antiheretical, they contain positive statements which include
the following points: (a) Jesus Christ, (b) son of Mary and
descended from Joseph, (c) miraculously generated by the
Holy Spirit, (d) truly born and living a genuine human life,
(e) crucified under Pontius Pilate (and Herod the tetrarch),
(f) raised from the dead. Any information about these matters *could* have come to Ignatius from credal formulas rather
than from books or more detailed traditions.

But in what Ignatius tells about Jesus there is considerably
more detail than could be derived from creeds.[14] There is
not only more detail, but more diversity—and the diversity
is present even in the passages which we have just treated
as semicredal. This means that the dogmatic tradition as
known to Ignatius is not absolutely fixed, at least at some
points. To put it another way, it would appear that he knows
various traditions, not just one.

It is clear that Ignatius does not feel compelled to mention
everything he knows every time he refers to particular items.
Thus he speaks fairly often of Christ's descent from Mary
and the Holy Spirit, but at points where he wants to lay
emphasis upon the human, fleshly aspects of the incarnate
Lord, he can refer only to Davidic descent (Trall. 9:1, Rom.

[14] For what follows cf. C. Maurer, *Ignatius von Antiochien und das
Johannesevangelium* (Zurich, 1949), 25-43; H. Koester, *Synoptische Über-
lieferungen bei den Apostolischen Vätern* (Berlin, 1957), 24-61; V. Corwin,
St. Ignatius and Christianity in Antioch (New Haven, 1960), 91-115.

7:3, Smyrn. 1:1). Similarly, when the humanity is being emphasized, Ignatius speaks of Jesus' being baptized to fulfill all righteousness (Smyrn. 1:1) but in a context in which something is being made of chrismation, baptism, and Eucharist (Eph. 17–20) the baptism took place for the cleansing of the water by the (future) passion (Eph. 18:2). In Ignatius' view one purpose does not exclude another. Similarly, in Trallians 9:2, where the humanity has just been emphasized, Ignatius speaks of the Father as having raised Jesus (imitating Pauline passages such as 2 Cor. 4:14 and Rom. 6:4-5); in Smyrnaeans 2 "he truly raised himself," a parallel to "he truly suffered" and related to John 10:17-18. This is to say that at one point Ignatius can follow one aspect of the Christian tradition and/or literature, at another point, another aspect. He is not bound to be Pauline or Johannine or anything else by itself.

What else does he know of, or in relation to, the apostolic tradition? When Jesus was born "a star shone forth in heaven" and its appearance had cosmic consequences (Eph. 19:2-3). Jesus had disciples or apostles (Magn. 13:2), among them not only Peter but also Paul (Rom. 4:3). To the apostles he gave ordinances (Magn. 13:1) or commandments (Eph. 9:2; Magn. 4:1; Rom. inscr.; Philad. 1:2) or a law (Magn. 2:1). He was a teacher (Eph. 15:1; Magn. 9:1-2; 10:1), and among the things he taught, probably, was the saying about being wise as a serpent and guileless as a dove (Polyc. 2:2). We may perhaps suppose that he also spoke about his Eucharistic flesh and blood (Rom. 7:3), about his being the door (Philad. 9:1), and about his pleasing him who sent him (Magn. 8:2). But he was no ordinary teacher. He was inextricably united with the Father (Eph. 5:1; Magn. 7:1), though he imitated the Father (Philad. 7:2) and was subject to him (Magn. 13:2). He was the Father's Word (Magn. 8:2) or even the Father's mouth (Rom. 8:2). He was not only Son of God but also Son of man (Eph. 20:2). He suffered for our sake (Trall. 2:1; Rom. 6:1) or "for our sins" (Smyrn. 7:1) or so that we

might attain salvation (Smyrn. 7:1). His cross and passion
were to provide resurrection for us (Smyrn. 5:3) or for all
(Eph. 9:1); the cross was the new tree of life, an ensign for
all nations (Smyrn. 1:2; cf. Trall. 11:2). He rose on the Lord's
Day (Magn. 9:1). He appeared in the flesh to Peter and
others and ate and drank with them (Smyrn. 3:2-3; 7:1).
He raised the Old Testament prophets from the dead (Magn.
9:2). Originally imperceptible and impassible, he became
passible for us but is now impassible again (Polyc. 3:2;
Smyrn. 3; Eph. 7:2).

If one asks what the origin of this information is, it seems
undeniable that the simplest, most obvious, and most convincing answer is that it comes from the tradition of the
church—a tradition complex, not uniform, and related primarily to the kinds of traditions found in the Gospels of
Matthew and John.

Of the various names of Jesus current in his time, Ignatius
uses "Jesus Christ" by far the most often. On ten occasions
he uses "Christ Jesus," once when mentioning Paul (Eph.
12:2), six times when alluding to the Pauline epistles (Trall.
9:2; Rom. 1:1, 2:2, 6:1; Philad. 10:1, 11:2), and three times
when mentioning the characteristically Pauline word "grace"
(Eph. 11:1; Magn. inscr., 8:2).[15] The name "Jesus" occurs
alone three times, twice in references to his earthly ministry
(Eph. 15:2; Philad. 5:1) but once in regard to his union with
the Father (Magn. 1:2). "Christ" is found only in the expression "the blood of Christ" (Smyrn. 1:1, 6:1). The phrase
"Jesus the Christ" (elsewhere only in 1 Clem. 42:1), appears
only once (Eph. 18:2), in apposition to "our God." Ignatius
may well have in mind something like John 7:42, where it is
stated that "the Christ" is "of the seed of David," since he
immediately proceeds to mention the Davidic ancestry.

Some of the titles or epithets Ignatius uses are rather unusual. Thus in Magnesians 8:2 he speaks of Jesus Christ as

[15] The same use of "Christ Jesus" occurs in 1 Clem. 32:4 and 38:1; the
name is not found elsewhere in the Apostolic Fathers.

God's "Word who came forth from silence"; the term *logos* is Johannine but Ignatius' mention of silence is either intended to emphasize the newness of revelation (cf. Eph. 19:1) or based on semi-Gnostic ideas of God as Silence. The former explanation seems correct. Again, in Romans 8:2 he refers to Christ as the "mouth" through which the Father spoke. Parallels to this expression occur in the semi-Gnostic *Odes of Solomon* (12:11) and *Gospel of Truth* (p. 26, 34); but the expression is not necessarily Gnostic.

Ignatius makes frequent use of the traditional or customary titles of Jesus Christ; of these, by far the most frequent is the title "Lord," while second is "God." Only occasionally does he use terms like "Savior," "Son of God," "Son of Man," "Teacher," "Physician," "High Priest," "Door," "Word," or "Beloved." These titles, it is fairly evident, can be traced back to the Church of New Testament times. The most significant of them is the appellation "God," which Ignatius employs far more often than any other early Christian writer.

In the New Testament there are five passages in which Jesus is clearly spoken of as God. Two of them occur in the Gospel of John. In John 1:1 the pre-existent Logos or Word of God is definitely designated "God,"[16] and similarly in John 20:28 the apostle Thomas hails the risen Jesus as "my Lord and my God." Other examples occur in Hebrews 1:8-9, Titus 2:13,[17] and 2 Peter 1:1.

There are fourteen such passages in the letters of Ignatius.

Eph. inscr.	"Jesus Christ our God"
1:1	"the blood of God"
7:2	"in man, God"
15:3	"our God in us"
17:2	"knowledge of God, which is Jesus Christ"
18:2	"our God Jesus the Christ"

[16] On the translation see E. C. Colwell in *Journal of Biblical Literature* 52 (1933), 12-21.

[17] See C. Spicq, *Les épîtres pastorales* (Paris, 1947), 265; B. S. Easton, *The Pastoral Epistles* (New York, 1947), 94-95.

19:3	"God was manifest as man"
Trall. 7:1	"God Jesus Christ"
Rom. inscr.	"Jesus Christ our God" (twice)
3:3	"our God Jesus Christ"
6:3	"the passion of my God"
Smyrn. 1:1	"Jesus Christ the God who . . ."
Polyc. 8:3	"our God Jesus Christ"

Such expressions thus occur in five of the seven Ignatian letters. Their absence from those to the Magnesians and the Philadelphians can be explained as due to Ignatius' awareness of the danger of Judaizing in the communities addressed. He does not feel free to use an expression which might provoke difficulty with Christians close to Judaism or Judaizers.

Ignatius uses this kind of language at the beginning and the end of some of his letters in setting forth the faith he shares with his readers (Eph. inscr.; Rom. inscr.; Polyc. 8:3), as well as in semicredal summaries (Eph. 7:2, 18:2, 19:3; Smyrn. 1:1). He also relates the deity of Jesus Christ to the life of Christians in the Church (Eph. 15:3, 17:2; Trall. 7:1; cf. Rom. inscr.; Smyrn. 1:1). Finally, the idea is expressed in relation to the passion of Jesus (Eph. 1:1; Rom. 6:3) or to his ascended life (Rom. 3:3).

Yet Ignatius has a firm grasp on the humanity of Jesus as well as his deity. "There is one physician, fleshly and spiritual, in man God, in death true life, both of Mary and of God, first passible and then impassible, Jesus Christ our Lord" (Eph. 7:2). He was "of the family of David after the flesh, Son of God in accordance with the will and power of God" (Smyrn. 1:1; cf. Paul, Rom. 1:3-4). Ignatius is aware that this teaching is paradoxical, and he sets forth the paradox as vividly as possible in his letter to Polycarp (3:2), where he calls Christ "the invisible one, visible for our sake; the intangible; the impassible, passible for our sake." His basic principle is expressed in Ephesians 19:3; "God was manifest as man." In Ephesians 20:2 he uses New Testament language in speaking of "Jesus Christ, after the flesh of the family of

David, Son of man and Son of God." The one who existed
"before the ages with the Father" was "made manifest at
the end" (Magn. 6:1). He is God's Son and "his Word who
came forth from silence" (8:2).

Ignatius is the only one among the Apostolic Fathers who
refers to the virginal conception. Two points must be made
clear in regard to this fact. (1) Ignatius definitely uses the
conception and birth of Jesus from Mary against those who
denied the physical, historical reality of the incarnation.
Jesus was a man. He was descended from David and born
of Mary: all the passages about his birth contain these elements. (2) The Davidic descent and the birth from Mary
are not notions invented by Ignatius but are traditional data,
perhaps already expressed in brief credal formulas, which
he could use against his opponents.

Like some of his contemporaries and some later writers,
Ignatius evidently believes that Mary was descended from
David. This point is evident when he speaks of Jesus' origin
"from the seed of David and the Holy Spirit" (Eph. 18:2)
and when he treats the two sources as analogous (Smyrn.
1:1). In the latter passage he seems to be relying on Paul's
expressions in Romans 1:3-4 and adding to them a (traditional) remark about the Virgin Mary.

In Ignatius' belief, Mary was not only a human being of
Davidic descent, to whom was due the human nature of
Jesus (Eph. 7:2)—so that he was Son of man as well as Son
of God (Eph. 20:2)—but also a virgin impregnated by the
Holy Spirit (Eph. 18:2). Just as the death of the Son of
God was mysterious and paradoxical, incomprehensible to
hostile spirits (Ignatius seems to rely on Paul's language in
1 Cor. 2:8), so the fact of Mary's virginity, along with the
fact of her giving birth, was a mystery to them. It was not
publicly known and it could not be publicly understood
(Eph. 19:1).

Ignatius lays tremendous emphasis upon the passion, the
cross, the blood, and the death of Jesus. The passion brings

peace to Christians (Trall. inscr.) and through it he calls
them as his members (11:2) so that they become the "fruit
of the cross" (Smyrn. 1:2) or "branches of the cross" (Trall.
11:2); they can be described as "nailed to the cross of the
Lord Jesus Christ" (Smyrn. 1:1). The cross, though a
stumbling block for unbelievers, is salvation and eternal life
for Christians (Eph. 18:1; cf. 1 Cor. 1:18). Therefore Christ's
blood can be described in terms of its effects, as imperishable
love (Rom. 7:3) or eternal and abiding joy (Philad. inscr.),
for it has confirmed Christians in their love (Smyrn. 1:1) and
kindled their proper task of charity (Eph. 1:1).

In the gospel "the passion has been revealed to us and
the resurrection has been accomplished" (Smyrn. 7:2); and
the passion is meaningful not only because it took place but
also because it is, since it brings about, our resurrection
(5:3). Christ suffered all these things on our account, so
that we might be saved (2:1). For this reason Ignatius
militantly defends the reality of the passion and the death of
Christ. If the passion was not real, Christian existence has
no reality (Trall. 10:1; Smyrn. 2:1, 4:2). It was the flesh of
our Savior Jesus Christ which suffered for our sins and was
raised by the Father (Smyrn. 7:1).

The way of the cross is to be followed by the Christian.
Ignatius calls upon his readers to "suffer together" (Polyc.
6:1) and to "choose to die through him in his passion"
(Magn. 5:2). Ignatius himself endures everything "in order
to suffer with him" (Smyrn. 4:2), for he desires to imitate the
passion of his God (Rom. 6:3). He accepts fire or cross or
other tortures if they await him (5:3), for his worldly desire
has already been crucified (7:2; cf. Gal. 2:19, 5:24). He is
willingly dying—on behalf of God (4:1).

Indeed, Ignatius views himself as a sacrificial offering
(antipsychon, cf. 4 Macc. 6:29) on behalf of other Christians
(Eph. 21:1; Smyrn. 10:2; Polyc. 2:3, 6:1). He is consecrated
on their behalf (Eph. 8:1; Trall. 13:3). He wants to be
"poured out to God while the altar is still ready" (Rom.
2:2). And he asks for the prayers of the various congrega-

tions so that by his suffering—being in bonds, fighting wild beasts, becoming the bread of God (ch. 4)—he may become a disciple, become a Christian, and finally "attain" to God or to Jesus Christ. He urges the Romans not to intercede for him and prevent his martyrdom, for he will "never have such an opportunity to attain to God" (2:1).

Behind his language there lies the idea of the imitation of God or of Christ (Eph. 1:1, 10:3; Rom. 6:3; Philad. 7:2) —primarily in suffering though also in other works of love. This idea is derived from the New Testament, where Paul too speaks of the imitation of God or of Christ or of himself (Eph. 5:1; I Cor. 11:1; Phil. 3:17; 1 Thess. 1:6; 2 Thess 3:7). It goes back to the synoptic tradition, according to which Jesus urges the disciple to take up his cross and follow him, to lose his life for his sake and that of the gospel, and not to gain the whole world and be deprived of life (Matt. 16:24ff.; Mark 8:34ff.; Luke 9:23ff.) Similarly, Ignatius says that it is better for him to die for Christ Jesus than to rule over the ends of the earth (Rom. 6:1). In Mark and Luke these sayings about discipleship are followed by the statement that when the Son of man comes he will not put to shame one who has not been ashamed of him and his words (or, according to some texts, his followers). Just so, Ignatius tells the Smyrnaeans that since they were not ashamed of his bonds, Jesus Christ will not put them to shame (10:2).

In addition, Ignatius' sacrificial language is based partly on 4 Maccabees but more significantly on Paul's letters. His word about being "poured out" recalls that of Paul in Philippians 2:17 (cf. 2 Tim. 4:6). Like Ignatius, Paul is eager to know Christ and the power of his resurrection and fellowship in his sufferings, and he denies that he has already attained or has been made perfect; he is pressing forward to the goal (Phil. 3:10-14). Paul rejoices in his sufferings on behalf of Christians, and he fills up what is lacking in the tribulations of Christ, in his own flesh on behalf of Christ's body, the Church (Col. 1:24).

The center of Ignatius' devotion and doctrine thus lies in

the New Testament, not in his psychological peculiarities or the influence of Gnostic ideas. He has a clear conception of his role as martyr and he calls upon other Christians to aid him in performing it. It is potentially the role of every Christian, for when he receives the pure light of God, he will become "a man"—what man was destined to be. Whoever has Christ in himself, he says, "must understand what I wish and sympathize with me" (Rom. 6:2-3). This is by no means to say that Ignatius wishes to become either the Christ or a Christ. He will become a disciple of "the new man Jesus Christ" (Eph. 20:1); "in the name of Jesus Christ I endure everything in order to suffer with him, since the perfect Man himself gives me strength" (Smyrn. 4:2).

These passages, chiefly reflecting Pauline ideas, prove that Harnack was wrong when he said that in the early Church only Marcion understood—and half-understood—Paul.

D. Hermas

The theology of Hermas is essentially Jewish, and it is very close to that of Clement. The first of Hermas' Mandates requires belief "that God is one, who created all things and perfected them, and made all things to be out of what was not, and contains all things, himself alone being uncontained." The picture of the creative act (Vis. 1, 3, 4) should be compared with that in 1 Clement 33.

1 Clement	*Hermas*
. . . by his all-powerful might he established the heavens and by his incomprehensible understanding he adorned them; he separated the earth from the water surrounding it and established it on the secure foundation of his will . . .	. . . by his mighty power and great understanding he created the universe and by his glorious counsel he provided his creation with beauty; by his mighty word he fixed the heaven and founded the earth upon the waters . . .

Both these pictures, however they may be related to each

other, are based on the beginning of Genesis as interpreted in Hellenistic Jewish circles.

The same observation may be made of what Hermas says of the work of the six principal angels. "These are the holy angels of God who were created first, to whom the Lord delivered all his creation to make it increase and to build it up and to rule over the whole creation" (Vis. 3, 4, 1).

Older than the angels, however, is the Son of God—older than all his creation, and counselor to the Father (Sim. 9, 12, 2). His name is great and incomprehensible, and it bears up the whole world (9, 14, 5).

Hermas has considerable difficulty in explaining the relationship of the Son to the angels. In Similitudes 8, 3 he says that God's law is God's Son, and the law is put into men's hearts by the great and glorious angel Michael. Again, in Similitudes 9, 1 the Holy Spirit is the Son of God. It need hardly be said that confusion of this kind results in confusion about the incarnation.

The incarnation is described thus (Sim. 5, 6): God made the Holy Spirit dwell in the flesh which he chose, and this flesh served the Spirit well; therefore God chose the flesh as a fellow (koinōnos) of the Spirit and gave it a place of tabernacling. The Son and the glorious angels were God's counselors in this decision. Hermas' statements are supposed to be exegesis of a parable he has told (Sim. 5, 2), in which the servant (explained as "flesh") becomes a joint heir with the son. Yet in Similitudes 5, 5 the servant is the Son of God.

The Spirit—the Holy Spirit, the divine Spirit, or the Spirit of the Deity—is especially effective in the work of revelation and is given to true prophets (Mand. 11). It is also present in all Christians and must be preserved undefiled (Sim. 5, 7).

Chapter VI

THE CHURCH: UNITY, MINISTRY, WORSHIP, DAILY LIFE

The primary theme with which most of the Apostolic Fathers are concerned is that of the community of God and its unity, expressed in its ministry and its worship. Clement and Ignatius write explicitly in order to ensure this unity; Polycarp and the Didachist give instructions about church life; 2 Clement is a sermon given in a church; Hermas receives a vision of the pre-existent Church; even Barnabas, though a private teacher, implies its existence as the context of his teaching.

In order to see what the Apostolic Fathers have to say about the Church and its life, we shall begin with their explicit doctrines and then pass on to what they say about its unity, its ministry, and the life of Christians.

I. Conceptions of the Church

Some of the more vividly imaginative ideas about the Church in the Apostolic Fathers are to be found among those who represent a kind of Jewish Christianity, and we therefore begin with them before turning to the ideas of Ignatius and then going on to the Church's unity.

According to the Shepherd of Hermas, one of God's first works was his creation of the pre-existent holy Church, "which he also blessed" (Vis. 1, 3, 4). It may well be that Hermas is giving an exegesis of Genesis 1:28, according to which God blessed the archetypal human being, both male and female, which he had created on the sixth day. The church is very old because she was created "first of all"; indeed, the world was established for her sake (Vis. 2, 4, 1)—just as in contemporary Jewish thought the world was established for the pre-existent Israel.[1]

Hermas also uses the image of a tower being built upon the water of baptism by six angels of God (Vis. 3, 3, 3–3, 4, 1). This image, more fully developed in the Ninth Similitude, is used to show how the Church is not only old but also new. In the last days she is becoming what she was originally created to be.

The pre-existent Church is also discussed in 2 Clement 14, where we read that the "first Church" is the spiritual one which was created before sun and moon; this is the "Church of life," and the body of Christ. Here the author relies either on Ephesians 5:23-30 (as is likely) or upon a similar tradition. He explains that the "male and female" of Genesis 1:27 refers to Christ and the Church. Just as Jesus, originally spiritual, was made manifest in the last days, so the Church, also spiritual, was made manifest "in the flesh of Christ" in order to save us. Jesus is prefigured by the "male" in Genesis and identified with the Spirit; the Church is prefigured by the "female" and identified with the flesh. This seems to imply that just as Jesus Christ became incarnate, so the Church became incarnate. Certainly the author elsewhere stated the first point: "Christ, the Lord who saved us, though he was originally spirit, became flesh and so called us" (9:5). Probably he maintained the second point as well.

Hermas and 2 Clement are among the more Jewish of the Apostolic Fathers, and in their writings we expect to find the Church related to God's purpose in terms of exegesis of Genesis. Such is also the case in what we know of Papias; according to the late writers who knew his work, he interpreted the beginning of Genesis in relation to Christ and

[1] See J. Daniélou, *Théologie du Judéo-Christianisme* (Tournai, 1958), 317-326.

the Church. Such notions are also reflected even in the letters of Ignatius, where the Church seems to be compared with the garden of Eden. It is possible that, as at other points, Ignatius' language reflects the earlier, more Jewish atmosphere of tradition at Antioch.

Practically nothing is said of the nature of the Church by Polycarp or Barnabas or in the Didache, and we therefore turn to the more theological discussions of Clement and Ignatius.

Since Clement is writing because of discord in the Corinthian community, we might expect that he would use the word "church" often. He does not do so. In 1 Clement it occurs twice in the salutation of the letter: "The Church of God which sojourns in Rome to the Church of God which sojourns in Corinth," and later on we hear of "the most steadfast and ancient church of the Corinthians" (47:6). Presbyters have been appointed "with the consent of the whole church" (44:3). Elsewhere two other terms are favored. One is the Pauline "body" (37:5, 38:1, 46:7). The other is "flock" (*poimnion*), also found in Acts 20:28 and I Peter 5:2-3. This word always occurs in the expression "flock of Christ." Christ belongs to those who are humble-minded, not to those who exalt themselves over his flock (16:1). Presbyters serve the flock of Christ (44:3), which must be at peace with the presbyters in charge of it (54:2). It is better to be insignificant but honorable in this flock than to be seemingly important and to be cast out from Christ's hope (57:2). The appearance of the word is all the more surprising because Clement does not refer to ministers as shepherds or to their function as shepherding. Presumably, then, the expression is traditional; he uses it because it points toward the aspect of the Church most neglected at Corinth.

The most complete description of the theological situation of the Church is to be derived from the descriptions of the churches in the salutations of Ignatius' letters. From these we learn that the Church is blessed and beloved by God and has obtained mercy from him, above all through the grace of God as expressed in the passion and resurrection of Jesus Christ. To God's grace the Church responds by obedience to him—by imitating him, by avoiding heresy, and by maintaining union with the bishops and other ministers. Only the church at Tralles is called "holy"—a word Ignatius elsewhere uses of the Spirit, of the Old Testament Holy of Holies, and of men through whom the Spirit works.

As in the book of Acts (cf. 4:32) the local church is called a "multitude," especially as contrasted with individuals within it. Ignatius says that he has seen the whole "multitude" when he has seen its representatives (Eph. 1:3; Magn. 6:1; Trall. 1:1); he contrasts the "multitude" with a few fools within it (Trall. 8:2). It is in this sense of an entire group that he also uses the word "catholic" or "whole." "Wherever the bishop appears, there let the multitude come, just as wherever Jesus Christ is, there is the 'catholic' church" (Smyrn. 8:2). So also episcopal direction at Antioch is provided, in Ignatius' absence, by Jesus Christ and by the love of the Roman community, and God is their shepherd in his stead (Rom. 9:1). The word "shepherd" occurs in the letters only here and in an analogous passage (Philad. 2:1). "Where the shepherd is, there follow as sheep."

Ignatius uses Pauline images when he describes the Church; he speaks of "the one body" of Christ's Church, consisting of both Jews and gentiles (Smyrn. 1:2) and refers to Christians as "members" of God's Son (Eph. 4:2)—members united with him as members of a body to its head or as a bride to a husband (Polyc. 5:1). Christians individually constitute "temples" (Eph. 15:3). Paul speaks of baptism into the one body for Jews and Greeks in 1 Corinthians 12:13 (cf. Eph. 2:16), of "the body of the church" in Colossians 1:18, of Christ as the bride in Ephesians 5:22ff., and of Christians at temples in 1 Corinthians 3:16 and 6:19. It is fairly clear that the epistles which have influenced Ignatius most are 1 Corinthians and Ephesians.

His images are not exclusively Pauline, however. In Trallians 11 (cf. Smyrn. 1:2), he speaks of Christians as "branches of the cross" planted by the Father and producing imperishable fruit. Here two figures of speech seem to be combined. First is the Johannine idea of Christ as the vine and the disciples as his branches (John 15:5), and of Christ as the vine, the Father as the one who planted it and cares for it (15:1). Second is, apparently, the identification of the Church with the garden of Eden and of the cross with the tree of life—as in Barnabas 11:6-8.

Whereas the Church was planted by the Father, there are also "evil weeds which Jesus Christ does not tend because they are not the planting of the Father" (Philad. 3:2). Ignatius urges the Ephesians (10:3) not to let a "plant of the devil" be found among them, and instructs the Trallians (11:1) to flee from evil offshoots which bear deadly fruit; if a man tastes it, he dies (cf. Gen. 2:17, of the tree of knowledge). The idea of plants not planted by the Father may come from Matthew 15:13; the idea that they were planted by the devil reminds one of the tares sown by the devil, according to Matthew 13:39.

II. The Unity of the Church

The most important aspect of the Church for the Apostolic Fathers is its unity. This unity is explicitly advocated by Clement and Ignatius, mentioned by Hermas and in the Didache, and implied by the words of Polycarp and Barnabas and in 2 Clement.

Clement's whole letter to the Corinthians is written in order to restore the lost unity of the Corinthian church by terminating the "strife and passions and divisions and schisms and even war" (46:5) in the community. Clement reminds his readers that Christians have "one God and one Christ and one Spirit of grace poured out" upon them, as well as "one calling in Christ" (46:6). For this reason he insists

upon the importance of orderliness within the community
(chs. 37-38, 40-44).

For Ignatius the unity of the Church is comparable to the
unity of Christ with the Father. In it there must be "one
prayer, one supplication, one mind, one hope in love."
Christians are to come together "as to one temple of God,
as to one sanctuary, to one Jesus Christ, who came forth
from the one Father and is with the one and departed to the
one" (Magn. 7). They are to "use one Eucharist, for the flesh
of our Lord Jesus Christ is one, and the cup for union with
his blood is one; there is one sanctuary, as there is one
bishop" (Philad. 4). Through Ignatius himself the Spirit
said, "Love unity and flee from divisions" (Philad. 7:2).
"Flee from divisions as the chief among evils" (Smyrn. 7:2).
Ignatius' insistence upon the importance of the bishop is due
to the belief that union with him is comparable to the unity
of the believer with Christ and that of Christ with the
Father.[2]

Similarly, in the most elaborate of the Similitudes of
Hermas we read that "those who believe in the Lord through
his Son and put on these spirits of virtue will become one
spirit and one body" (Sim. 9, 13, 5). After evildoers have
been expelled, "the Church of God will be one body, one
understanding, one mind, one faith, one love, and then the
Son of God will rejoice and be glad in them" (9, 18, 4);
this will take place after believers have received "the seal"
(9, 17, 4).[3]

Can the ideas of Clement, Ignatius, and Hermas be traced
back to earlier Christian thought? It seems quite certain that
they can. Clement explicitly refers to Paul's (first) letter to
the Corinthians as his principal guide (47:1) and clearly
makes use of ideas expressed in it as well as in Ephesians.
Similarly, Ignatius knows and uses both Corinthians and

---

[2] The noun for unity occurs eleven times in Ignatius' letters, the verb six
times; neither is found elsewhere among the Apostolic Fathers.

[3] On the seal cf. A. Benoit, *La baptême chrétien au second siècle* (Paris,
1953), 100-110; 131-132.

Ephesians and, in addition, either the Gospel of John or oral tradition derived from the evangelist. The expressions employed by Hermas almost certainly come from Ephesians 4:4-6. This is to say that at Rome the ideas about unity are primarily Pauline in origin, while at Antioch and in Asia Minor they reflect both Paul and John—the apostles of unity. In any event, all alike come from earlier Christian sources.

The Didache looks toward unity by insisting upon a common catechism (chs. 1–6), common liturgical practices (chs. 7–10), a common ministry (chs. 11–15), and a common hope (ch. 16). No explicit mention of unity is provided, but Christians pray for the gathering together of the Church from the ends of the earth into God's kingdom (9:4) or its being made perfect in God's love and, when sanctified, being gathered together from the four winds (10:5). No one is to participate in the Eucharist unless he has been baptized (9:5) and has been reconciled with his neighbor (14:2).

In common with Ignatius (Polyc. 4:2; cf. Eph. 13:1) and 2 Clement (17:3) the Didachist recommends frequent Christian assemblies. Gathering together expresses and increases unity at the same time.

Polycarp says little about unity directly, since it does not seem to have been immediately threatened in the Philippian community. He does state that Christians should avoid "the false brethren and those who bear the Lord's name in hypocrisy" (6:3), while they are to be "loving the brotherhood, affectionate toward one another, joined together in the truth, giving preference to one another in the gentleness of the Lord" (10:1). These positive counsels recall 1 Peter 2:17 ("love the brotherhood"), Romans 12:10 ("affectionate toward one another in the brotherhood, in honor giving preference to one another"), and 2 Corinthians 10:1 ("I exhort you through the . . . gentleness of Christ"). Specifically, in regard to the presbyter Valens and his wife (11:4), the community should not treat them as enemies (cf. 2. Thess. 3:15) but recall them as members—though frail and aberrant—in order to preserve the body of them all. By so doing they will build themselves up (cf. 1 Cor. 14:3).

Polycarp's ideas are largely Pauline, as the references given above suggest. In addition, he knows 1 Clement practically by heart, and the idea of "preserving the whole body" is one which Clement mentions twice in the course of his appeals for unity (37:5, 38:1). Because of this close connection we may assume that had Polycarp discussed unity more fully, he would have continued to follow the lines laid down in the Pauline epistles and in 1 Clement.

The views of Barnabas about unity are less clearly expressed. They occur largely in contexts in which Barnabas is criticizing the literal interpretation of the Jewish law and urging Christians to avoid it. He does state, however, that God prepared a people—the Church—in his Beloved (3:6); this is the only people to whom the covenant belongs (4:7). Jesus and the Church are closely related (7:11), and Christians become a spiritual temple for the Lord (ch. 16). But Barnabas develops none of these themes. Perhaps the reason for his relative lack of concern for unity lies in his position as a private teacher dealing with allegorical exegesis (9:9).[4] It should perhaps be added that both Polycarp (7:2) and Papias (Eusebius, *H. E.* 3, 39, 3) speak of "the many" as contrasted with their own adherents. In the view of Walter Bauer the term implied that both of these "orthodox" leaders represented minorities among the Christians of Asia Minor.[5]

Such a theory is, of course, possible; but it seems unlikely that the expression "the many" (*hoi polloi*) has to be taken so literally. It conveys a value judgment as much as, and perhaps more than, a statistical estimate. It is aristocratic as against the writers' inferiors, and it is used in order to suggest that their readers belong with them against their opponents.

---

[4] He never uses the word "one" of the unity of Christians.

[5] *Rechtgläubigkeit und Ketzerei im ältesten Christentum* (Tübingen, 1934).

For most of the Apostolic Fathers the question of unity was closely related to the question of ministerial authority, and for this reason we must now turn to their views of the ministry. Before doing so, however, we shall briefly examine the New Testament evidence about the ministry, for the Apostolic Fathers did not create the ministry; they believed that they were reflecting the purpose of Christ and his apostles by maintaining it.

III. The Ministry

A. The Apostolic Ministry in the Letters of Paul

The most obvious point at which to begin our consideration of the New Testament ministry lies in the salutations of the Pauline epistles. While in the salutations of the Thessalonian letters, Philippians, and Philemon, Paul does not refer to himself as an apostle, he does so in the Corinthian letters, Galatians, Romans, Colossians, and Ephesians; and the expressions he uses cast some light on what he means by the term. In both Corinthian letters he speaks of himself as "called to be an apostle by the will of God"; in Galatians he says that he is an "apostle not from men or through a man but through Jesus Christ and God the Father who raised him from the dead"; and in Romans he states that he was "called to be an apostle, set apart for the gospel of God, which was proclaimed in advance through his prophets in holy scriptures, concerning his Son—through whom we received grace and the apostolate for the obedience of faith among all the gentiles on behalf of his name." The gradually developing fullness of Paul's expressions deserves notice, especially since in the Thessalonian letters, written in the names of Paul and Silvanus and Timothy, the term "apostle" does not occur in the salutation. At Thessalonica the apostolic office of Paul and his colleagues was not in question; they were the ones who first proclaimed the gospel to the Thessalonians (1 Thess. 2:2, 8); they were "apostles of Christ" (2:6). "Our brother" Timothy, though obviously subordinate to Paul, who could send him on a mission (3:2), could thus be regarded as an apostle in the inclusive sense of the term (cf. Acts 16:3), as could the Jerusalem prophet Silvanus-Silas (Acts 15:32). It is in the later letters, which reflect or sum up controversies about the apostolate, that Paul insists upon the uniqueness of his office.

From the salutations, then, we learn that (1) Paul's insistence upon his unique apostolate developed only gradually, and (2) earlier he used the term in a more general sense.

In 1 Corinthians we find Paul as an apostle differentiating himself from others. The letter is written in the name of "Paul, . . . called to be an apostle of Jesus Christ, and our brother Sosthenes." Sosthenes, presumably the former head of the Corinthian synagogue mentioned in Acts 18:17, is not an apostle but a brother, even though he presumably has some relation of authority in regard to the Corinthians. Paul carefully states that he is an apostle and that he has seen the Lord; the Corinthian church itself is the proof (*sphragis*, "seal") of his apostolate (9:1-2). Because he is an apostle, he has the right to take a Christian wife with him on his missionary journeys—"like the rest of the apostles and the brethren of the Lord and Cephas" (9:5). Since Cephas (the Aramaic name of Peter) is obviously an apostle, as is James the Lord's brother (Gal. 1:19), presumably Paul's sentence means "the rest of the apostles, such as the brethren of the Lord and Cephas." Then when he goes on to ask, ironically, whether only he and Barnabas do not possess the right not to work, he must be comparing two groups of apostles; therefore in his view Barnabas too was an apostle. It is not clear how Barnabas came to be an apostle. In 1 Corinthians 15:5-11 Paul associates himself with the other apostles and suggests that all were called by the risen Lord.

> He appeared to Cephas,
> then to the Twelve,

then he appeared to more than five hundred brethren at once,
    (most of whom still survive, though some have fallen asleep);
then he appeared to James,
        then to all the apostles;
last of all, as to an abortion, he appeared also to me.

I am the least of the apostles;
I am unworthy to be called an apostle,
for I persecuted the Church of God.

But by God's grace I am what I am,
    and his grace toward me was not in vain,
but I worked harder than all of them—
not I, but the grace of God with me.
Whether they or I,
        so we preach and
        so you believed.

This passage is significant not only for its co-ordination of resurrection appearance with the apostolate (Cephas and the Twelve; James and all the apostles) but also for the association of appearances with a vocation to labor in the apostolic work of preaching the gospel. The grace of God expressed in an appearance of the risen Lord *could* be fruitless; but apostolate implies performance. It implies mission. Not everyone who saw the risen Lord became an apostle. Had the "five hundred brethren" become apostles, we could hardly understand why Paul was as insistent upon his own office as he was.

Such questions as those concerning the precise identification of the various resurrection appearances and the origins of Paul's list are either unanswerable or irrelevant. The most natural explanation of the origin of the list is that Paul received it at Jerusalem from Cephas and James during the visit he mentions in Galatians 1:18-19.

The vocation of an apostle is an exalted one, and it originates with God. In the Church God established a hierarchical ministry, consisting of "first, apostles; second, prophets; third, teachers; then"—a list of activities presumably open to all (12:28)—including "miracle-workings, gifts of healing, assistances, governings, various kinds of ecstatic speech." But while all might conceivably prophesy (14:24)—and, *a fortiori*, perform other functions inferior to prophecy—only those chosen by God through the risen Lord could be apostles.

1 Corinthians clearly shows that Paul himself is the apostolic governor of the church. Yet just as at Thessalonica (1 Thess. 5:12), there is what we may call an improvised local ministry. Paul not only uses, or wants to use, the ambassadorial services of Timothy and Apollos (1 Cor. 16:10-12; in 2 Cor., Titus); he urges the Corinthians to be subordinate to the household of Stephanas, his first converts in Achaea (16:15-18; cf. 1:16), and others like them. From the letter it is not clear whether Paul is creating an office for Stephanas as he writes or is recalling the Corinthians to obedience. In either case the ultimate authority is Paul's own, as we see most clearly in his instructions about the excommunication of an offender from the community (1 Cor. 5:3-5).

In 2 Corinthians neither Sosthenes nor Stephanas is mentioned. The letter comes from the apostle Paul and brother Timothy, and reminds its readers of the proclamation at Corinth "through me and Silvanus and Timothy" (1:19). The main difficulty in the church, according to this letter, is due to "false apostles . . . transformed into apostles of Christ" (11:13). These men, evidently Jewish Christians (11:22), claim to be "ministers of Christ" (11:23) and are setting forth what Paul views as another Jesus, another Spirit, and another gospel (11:4). They compare Paul, to his disadvantage, with those whom he ironically calls "superlative apostles" (11:5; 12:11). He argues that he is in no way inferior to such men, and that his apostolate has been confirmed by his sufferings and by signs, wonders, and miracles (12:12).

There was evidently some tension between Paul and the Jerusalem church—already intimated in 1 Corinthians 15 and to be expressed openly in Galatians—and it would ap-

pear that, as von Campenhausen suggests, some visitors to
Corinth have tried to widen the breach.[6] There is no reason
to suppose that the troublemakers were apostles. When Paul
calls them "false apostles," his words hardly imply that they
really were apostles. But there is some difficulty related to
the division of spheres of missionary activity. Paul states
that, unlike his opponents, he works in the areas assigned to
him (10:13-16). What he means may become clearer when
we consider Galatians.

It is in Galatians that the whole conflict between Paul
and some leaders of the Jerusalem church comes to the sur-
face. Missionaries from Jerusalem have apparently invaded
his mission area in Galatia and have been urging gentiles
to become circumcised. Paul regards their activity as a viola-
tion not only of his apostolic authority, but also of the agreement he has already reached with the Jerusalem leaders. In
the first two chapters of Galatians he is trying to demonstrate
his complete independence from the Jerusalem church. He
is an apostle "not from men or through a man but through
Jesus Christ and God the Father" (1:1). He did not receive
his gospel from a man nor was he taught it; it came to him
through a revelation from Jesus Christ (1:12).

> When he who set me apart before my birth and called me
> through his grace chose to reveal his Son in me, so that I
> might proclaim him among the gentiles, the first thing I did
> was not to consult with any human being or to go up to
> Jerusalem, to those who were apostles before me, but to go
> away to Arabia. . . . Then after three years I went up to
> Jerusalem to confer with Cephas, and I stayed with him
> for a fortnight; I saw none of the other apostles, except
> James the Lord's brother (1:15-19).

Much later, fourteen years after his conversion, he went up
to Jerusalem with Barnabas, taking Titus along too; he went

---

[6] H. von Camphenhausen, *Kirchliches Amt und Geistliche Vollmacht in
den drei ersten Jahrhunderten* (Tübingen, 1933), 34.

up because of a revelation, not because the Jerusalem apostles invited him to come (2:1).

> I set before them the gospel which I preach among the gentiles, but privately, before the authorities, so that I would not run or have run in vain. . . . The authorities laid no further requirements upon me; on the contrary, recognizing that I have been entrusted with the gospel for the uncircumcision, as Peter has been entrusted with the gospel for the circumcision—for he who worked in Peter, for the apostolate to the circumcision, also worked in me for the gentiles—and being aware of the grace which was given me, James and Cephas and John, who seem to be "pillars," gave me and Barnabas their right hands [in token of] fellowship, so that we might go to the gentiles, they to the circumcision. The only requirement they made was that we should remember "the poor"—a task I was eager to undertake (2:2, 6-10).

This account seems to set forth not only the exemption of gentile converts from the requirement of circumcision but also the differentiation of areas of mission work. It can hardly be accidental that after Paul's first visit to Jerusalem he went "to the regions of Syria and Cilicia" and took no part in the work of the Jerusalem church or of other Judaean churches (1:21-24). His departure for Syria and Cilicia may have been in part a matter of convenience, since according to Acts 9:28-30 he had aroused the hostility of Jewish "Hellenists" in Jerusalem; but it prepared the way for a fairly clear differentiation of Jewish and gentile missions. This differentiation was made explicit during his second visit to Jerusalem. Paul's account in Galatians suggests that the Jerusalem church was governed by three "pillars," only one of whom was actively concerned with mission work. This one, Peter, was the director of missions among Jews, though James the Lord's brother and John the son of Zebedee obviously co-operated with him. At the council, mission work among gentiles was given semiautonomous status. Paul and

Barnabas were to be completely responsible for work among the gentiles, though they were to take up a collection among their converts for the support of the poor in the Jerusalem church, thus binding the two kinds of communities together.

Such a sharp distinction between Jewish and gentile Christians was undoubtedly useful as far as the interrelations of administrators were concerned. It was not so useful when practical problems arose in the mission fields, for in most of the cities of the East there were large communities of Jews who could hardly be neglected by missioners to the gentiles. Similarly, missions to the Jews could hardly be conducted without any reference to gentile Christians.

Conflict inevitably arose when Peter paid a visit to a community which was both Jewish and gentile, the church of Antioch. On the basis of the agreement Paul had made at Jerusalem, he was to go to the gentiles, Peter to the Jews. At Antioch, however, Jews disregarded the dietary laws and ate with gentiles, and Peter proceeded to adapt himself to local conditions by eating with both. Mindful of the Jewish mission, James thereupon sent messengers to remind Peter of his responsibilty for the Jews; Peter and the other Jews stopped eating with gentiles. It is not quite clear what Barnabas did (Gal. 2:13). Perhaps the most likely explanation is that he encouraged segregation and himself ate only with gentiles. Paul thereupon put his finger on the inconsistency of the Jerusalem agreement. He "said to Cephas before them all, 'If you, Jew that you are, live in gentile fashion, not Jewish, how is it that you are compelling the gentiles to live in Jewish fashion?'" (2:14). By the words "in Jewish fashion" he referred to the forced segregation at meals which, implicit in the Jerusalem agreement, was impossible under circumstances not envisaged by the agreement.

Since Paul had agreed to remain a missionary to the gentiles, it is difficult to see the logic of his irritation, though easy to see its emotional origin. When in 1 Corinthians 9:19-22 he describes his mission as one to Jews and gentiles alike, it is also easy to see how this might have been greeted at Jerusalem, and how the apostles might have suggested that he was not altogether reliable. The fact that Titus, a Greek, was not circumcised at Jerusalem (Gal. 2:3) is really irrelevant, except insofar as the Jerusalem apostles may have infringed on Paul's territory as he has infringed on theirs.

In all this account there is no suggestion that Paul was "ordained" an apostle, even though from Galatians 1:1 it would perhaps appear that there were those who thought he had been so ordained; but his insistence on his absolute independence does not necessarily imply that his opponents insisted on his equally absolute dependence. It is unlikely that they said he received his apostolate "from men." At Jerusalem the apostles were willing to acknowledge his apostolate because they had already acknowledged the apostolate of James the Lord's brother (Gal. 1:19) since Christ had appeared to him and apparently had commissioned him as an apostle (1 Cor. 15:7). What they would not acknowledge was the universality of Paul's apostolate. He was an apostle to the Corinthians, they would agree, but not to others (1 Cor. 9:2).

In Galatians there is no trace of a local ministry, perhaps because the letter is an encyclical to "the churches of Galatia" (1:2), perhaps because the local ministers have been led astray by Paul's opponents. No gospel different from his can be accepted even if it should be proclaimed by "an angel from heaven" (1:8).

In Romans, Paul's tone is less intense, though he begins by speaking of himself as "a slave of Christ Jesus, called to be an apostle and set apart (cf. Gal. 1:15) for the gospel of God" (1:1). Local ministers owe their ministry to gifts of grace (12:6-8); these ministries include prophecy, service (*diakonia*), teaching, exhortation, handing over (the tradition?), governing, and almsgiving. It would appear that Paul does not know just how the church of Rome is organized. To the Romans (if ch. 16 is really a part of this letter) Paul commends "Phoebe our sister, who is a deaconess (*diakonos*) of the church which is in Cenchreae" (Rom. 16:1). He also sends greetings to "Andronicus and Junias, my kinsmen and fellow prisoners, who are famous among the apostles and were before me in Christ" (16:7). Paul's expression can mean either that these two were apostles or that they were highly regarded by the apostles. In view of the other Pauline evidence, the latter interpretation is probably correct.

The imprisonment epistles provide further evidence concerning local ministers. Paul writes "to all the saints in Christ Jesus who are at Philippi, together with the bishops and deacons" (Phil. 1:1). No explanation of the work of these officers is provided. Perhaps the apostle had appointed them; perhaps the community had appointed them, as they had appointed Epaphroditus, "my fellow soldier, your apostle and minister to my need" (2:25). This use of the term "apostle" is different from Paul's ordinary use. Here he is referring to the fact that Epaphroditus had been sent as an emissary by the Philippian church, with funds for his assistance. It is worth noting that in writing to a community in which Paul's apostolate is not in question, he does not refer to himself as an apostle. Colossians too is a relatively quiet letter. Paul refers to himself as "an apostle of Christ Jesus through the will of God" (1:1), but he does not discuss the ministry except by asking the community to "say to Archippus, 'Watch out for the ministry (*diakonia*) which you have received in the Lord, so that you may fulfill it' " (4:17). Archippus, like the Philippian Epaphroditus, is Paul's "fellow soldier" (Philemon 2). Perhaps—though this is only a possibility—Archippus and Epaphroditus were bishops in their communities.

Finally, in Ephesians, which is certainly a Pauline epistle whether written by Paul or not, we find that the church was built on the foundation of the apostles and prophets (2:20) to whom the "mystery" of the unity of Jews and gentiles had been revealed (3:5-6). In the church God "gave apostles, prophets, evangelists, shepherds, and teachers" (4:11)—a list which recalls 1 Corinthians 12:28, though evangelists and shepherds have been inserted between prophets and teachers, presumably because of the development of the local ministry.

The apostolate in the Pauline epistles is primarily a vocation given by God through the risen Lord to those who proclaim the gospel. Not all who proclaim the gospel are apostles, but an apostle is one who has been "sent" (*apostellein*) and commissioned by God. The proof of his apostolate is provided by "signs, wonders, and miracles"; its authenticity is confirmed by the existence of Christian communities.

Chief among the apostles are Peter, responsible for the Jewish mission, and Paul, entrusted with that to gentiles. The fact that Paul was not a member of the original group of the Twelve may have made it difficult for the Jerusalem Christians to recognize his apostolate, but they had already recognized that of James the Lord's brother, who was not one of the Twelve either.

Exact definition of the apostolic office appears to have come only gradually, for in 1 Thessalonians Paul seems to refer to Timothy and Silvanus as apostles, and in Philippians the "apostle" of a local church is mentioned (Romans 16:7 is ambiguous, but its very ambiguity points to a lack of precise definition).

As a "sent" apostle, Paul could send others on missions to his churches; from Galatians it is evident that James too could employ such agents. The term "apostle," however, was generally reserved for the Twelve, James, Paul, and Barnabas.

B. The Apostolic Ministry in the Rest of the New Testament

In the earliest, and in what may be the latest, of the Gospels the term "apostle" is extraordinarily infrequent. In

Mark 6:30 the Twelve, who have been sent out on a mission, are described as "the apostles"; the term may mean no more than "those sent." It clearly bears this meaning in John 13:16, where we find the statement that "one sent" (*apostolos*) is not greater than the one who sent him. It is also very rare in Matthew; indeed, it appears only in a list (derived from Mark) of the Twelve; they are called "the twelve apostles" (Matt. 10:2).

This is to say only that the term is unusual. The idea of sending out a group of disciples, pre-eminently the Twelve, is fairly common. The disciples are sent out in Mark 3:14 and 6:7, as in Matthew 10:5, 16. The notion of sending is especially conspicuous in the Gospel of John, where both Jesus and the Paraclete are sent by the Father, and Jesus himself sends his disciples.

There is a special group known ordinarily as "the Twelve," as we learn from Mark (3:14-19; 6:7; 9:35; 10:32; 11:11; 14:10, 17, 43), Matthew (parallels to Mark), and John (6:67-71; 20:24). Matthew 19:28 (cf. Luke 22:30) assigns them an eschatological function: they will sit on thrones judging the twelve tribes of Israel. In view of Paul's reference to them in 1 Corinthians 15:5, their historical reality can hardly be doubted.

We should infer that there was a group of twelve which constituted the core of Jesus' disciples, but that the term "apostle" was not applied to them in any technical sense.

It is in Luke that we find the Twelve specifically identified as apostles. "He called his disciples, and he chose from them twelve, whom he also named apostles" (6:13). The existence of this group as a sharply delimited one is emphasized in Luke 22:3: Judas Iscariot was "of the number of the Twelve." Luke is apparently preparing the way for his account in Acts 1:21-26 concerning the selection of Matthias to take the place of Judas. The eleven chose two men who had been with Jesus during his earthly ministry; they prayed and cast lots, and the lot fell upon Matthias.

According to E. Haenchen[7] this account is quite unhistorical, for in his address to "the brethren" Peter refers to
the Aramaic name of the field owned by Judas as "in their
language"; he quotes Psalm verses from the Septuagint; and
apostles are supposed to have accompanied Jesus from his
baptism onward. These difficulties suggest that the account
is not reliable in every detail; they do not prove that the
event did not take place.

The Twelve are less important in Acts than in the Gospel
of Luke; as a group they are mentioned only in Acts 6:2 and,
by implication, in 1:26 and 2:14. On the other hand, we
often hear of "the apostles," and by this term Luke usually
means to indicate the Twelve (cf. Luke 6:13). According to
Acts 6:1-6, the Twelve directed the whole Jerusalem community to choose men to "serve tables," either as waiters or
as bankers, and the seven who were chosen were set "before
the apostles." The apostles followed the Jewish practice of
praying and laying hands upon them, thus ordaining and
empowering them for their special function. From Acts we
learn nothing about the origins of other orders of ministers at
Jerusalem. Many Jewish priests were converted to Christianity, according to Acts 6:7; but it is not said that they became Christian priests. It is obvious, however, that there were
various kinds of ministers at Jerusalem, including prophets
(11:27; 15:32; 21:10) and elders (11:30; 15:2, 6, 22-23;
21:18). Presumably Luke supposes that the elders were appointed by the apostles (cf. 14:28).

Luke's picture of the church of Antioch is not altogether
clear. After a preliminary period of independent missionary
activity, the Jerusalem church sent Barnabas to Antioch;
Barnabas brought Paul there; prophets also arrived from
Jerusalem (11:19-27). Of Barnabas, however, we learn only
that he gave his property to the apostles and was given his
name by them (4:36-37), and that he was among the
"prophets and teachers" of Antioch (13:1). The mission

[7] *Die Apostelgeschichte* (12th ed., Göttingen, 1959), 128.

work from Antioch began when five prophets and teachers fasted and were told by the Holy Spirit to "set apart" two among them—Barnabas and Paul—for the task. They fasted, prayed, and laid hands upon the two missionaries (13:2-3), who are then described as "sent out by the Holy Spirit" (13:4). It is after this point that Luke refers to them as "apostles" (14:4, 14) and says that "they appointed elders in various churches, and after prayer with fasting they set them apart for the Lord" (14:23). One must agree with Haenchen[8] that Luke's picture corresponds not with anything in the Pauline epistles but with Titus 1:5, which reflects the period in which Luke was writing. In his major epistles Paul never refers to elders.

Luke is convinced, however, that elders do exist in the gentile churches as well as at Jerusalem. On Paul's way back to Jerusalem he summons the elders of the church of Ephesus to meet him at Miletus (20:17) and tells them that the Holy Spirit has set them in the sheepfold as bishops (*episkopoi*) "to shepherd the Church of God" (20:28). As Haenchen says,[9] "a presbytery governs the individual communities; its members are called *episkopoi;* therefore in Luke's time the Presbyterian system, after a Jewish pattern, was predominant." This conclusion is correct. All elders were *episkopoi.*

One must conclude that Luke's picture of the apostolic ministry, both in his Gospel and in Acts, reflects some modification of the materials which we can compare with his statements. In Mark the apostolic *office* is by no means as clear as the apostolic *function.* In the Pauline epistles the elders do not have the relationship to the apostles which Luke gives them. Luke has consciously or unconsciously rewritten the history of the ministry in the light of what it has become in his time.

On the other hand, if we express doubts about the antiquity

[8] *Ibid.*, 377.
[9] *Ibid.*, 525.

of what Luke sets forth, we must still ask how it was that by Luke's time (A.D. 75-80) the ministry he describes had come into existence. If Paul did not ordain elders, were there not apostles who did so? Was the ministry of those who were not apostles a new creation?

The Pastoral letters were written either by the apostle Paul or, more probable, in his name to his lieutenants Timothy and Titus (Timothy is otherwise known from the major Pauline epistles and Acts, Titus only from the epistles). These letters are primarily concerned with "how men ought to behave themselves in the house of God" (1 Tim. 3:15) and therefore deal with such matters as heretical teaching and ministerial order.

There is a clear picture of apostolic succession in the letters. Prophecies—presumably by Christian prophets—led the way to the appointment of Timothy as Paul's assistant; he received a spiritual gift "by prophecy, with the laying on of hands of the presbytery" (1 Tim. 1:18; 4:14); in addition, Paul himself laid hands on him (2 Tim. 1:6). In turn, Timothy himself lays hands on others (1 Tim. 5:22), just as Titus appoints "elders in every city" (Titus 1:5).

The persons thus appointed and ordained are divided into two categories. Less significant are the deacons, including men and women alike (1 Tim. 3:8-13); more important are the elders or presbyters, who not only preach and teach but also can impose their hands on others (1 Tim. 5:17-22; 4:14). The presbyters who "rule well" are to be counted worthy of double honor (1 Tim. 5:17); presumably this honor is that of being given the office of overseer or bishop (1 Tim. 3:1-7; Tit. 1:7-9). The chain of ideas in Titus 1:5-9 shows conclusively that some elders, and perhaps all of them, were regarded as overseers; the same situation is reflected in Acts 20:17, 28. It is analogous to that implied in Philippians 1:1, where Paul speaks of "bishops and deacons." But presbyters are mentioned nowhere in the major Pauline epistles.

From these facts we should infer that in the time and

place in which the Pastorals were written—probably in Asia Minor not long after A.D. 70—the organization of the churches was gradually becoming more systematic. As Schniewind pointed out, however, the office of the deacon was not clearly defined;[10] and there was no sharp line dividing bishops and presbyters.

C.   The Role of the Prophets and Teachers

The early church arose in an environment in which great emphasis was laid on the fulfillment of Old Testament prophecy, and hence on prophecy as such. According to Jewish theory, prophecy had come to an end with Malachi, the last of the prophets. Its renewal was thus regarded as a sign that a new age had dawned. According to the Gospels, Jesus was regarded by some as a prophet, but this fact is not so important for our purposes as the awareness of the early Church that somehow it possessed the prophetic gift.

We shall examine the texts related to the Christian prophets in approximately the same order as those related to apostles, though there are fewer texts related to prophets than to the "regular ministry."

Paul's earliest extant letter, 1 Thessalonians, deals with the question of Christian prophecy but does not mention prophets. In 1 Thessalonians 5:19-21 he instructs his readers with these words: "Do not quench the Spirit, do not despise prophecy; but test everything and hold fast to what is good." Evidently the Thessalonian community is one in which there is a certain lack of enthusiasm for prophecy, perhaps related to the expectation of the Lord's coming which seems to be delayed (4:13–5:11). It may be that Christian prophets had predicted the Lord's coming prematurely; for this reason Paul explains that on the one hand the Lord will come, but on the other, his "day" will come like a thief in the night. If this is the true context of the Thessalonians' lack of interest in prophecy, we may perhaps infer that the test of prophecy

10 *Festschrift Rudolf Bultmann* (Stuttgart, 1949), 205.

is its fulfillment or lack of fulfillment, as in Deuteronomy 18:22; "what is good" is prophecy which is not too specific about "times and seasons."

This would mean that the prophets present in the Thessalonian community were essentially like the Jewish prophets or the Jewish-Christian prophets of the book of Acts (cf. Acts 11:27-28; 21:10-11).

The earliest texts we possess dealing with Christian prophets as such are to be found in 1 Corinthians, in which Paul is trying either to restore a lost order to the Corinthian community or to create an order which did not exist previously. His method of dealing with the Corinthians' problems seems to be one of gradually sharpening the rigor of his commands. Thus in chapter 8 he is more "permissive" in regard to meats offered to idols, while in chapter 10 he lays down definite rules. And in chapter 11 he sets forth conditions under which women may speak in church, while in chapter fourteen he forbids this practice. In other words, he starts where the Corinthians are and then tries to lead them to accept his own view.

Corinthian practice obviously permits both men and women to pray and to prophesy in church (11:4-5). It is not clear whether or not all Christians tried to prophesy (cf. 14:31); in any case, Paul's own view is that not all are prophets, just as not all are apostles or teachers (12:28-29). And he insists on the rational nature of prophecy as contrasted with ecstatic speech (14:15-19). "The spirits of the prophets are subordinate to the prophets" (14:32). Only two or three prophets are to speak, and one at a time (14:29-31). Everything is to be done "decently and in order" (14:40).

Paul makes a vigorous effort to distinguish prophecy from ecstatic speech and to show the superiority of prophecy (14:5). This effort suggests that the Corinthians regarded ecstatic speech as the climax of prophecy; it was a proof that "God was really among them" (cf. 14:25). For this reason

Paul lists various officers placed by God in the Church—apostles, prophets, teachers—and then adds various spiritual gifts, the last of which is ecstatic speech (12:28); the Corinthians are to "be zealous for the greater gifts" (12:31).

The logic of the chapters on spiritual gifts (chs. 12–14), however, leaves much to be desired. Paul has begun by pointing out that just as not all are apostles, not all are prophets (12:29). Then, after indicating the inferiority of prophecy to Christian love (13:2, 8), he urges all to "be zealous for spiritual gifts, especially so that you may prophesy" (14:1). One passage may be addressed particularly to the prophets: "Two or three prophets are to speak, and the others are to weigh what is said; if a revelation is made to another sitting by, the first is to be silent; for you can all prophesy in turn, so that all may learn and all may be encouraged" (14:20-31). For there are evidently some who regard themselves as prophets in the church (14:37), as Paul himself believes. How then can he conclude by urging them all once more to be zealous to prophesy (14:39)?

Unless we have recourse to the removal of inconvenient passages, we must assume that all Christians are potentially prophets, though only some are actually prophets. And in this respect there is a great difference between an apostle and a prophet. The apostolate, as we have said, is not a spiritual gift but a vocation. Prophecy, on the other hand, is not a vocation but a spiritual gift.

The trouble in Corinth arose because the prophets did not understand what the spiritual gift was which they had received. They inclined toward ecstatic speech, while Paul preferred to speak five words with his mind, to instruct others, to speaking countless words in ecstasy (14:19).

The "prophets" of Corinth are thus quite different from those of Thessalonica. Their primary function is ecstatic speech, not prediction. They edify themselves, not the church (14:4). And in an obscure sentence (12:2) Paul seems to

indicate that the origin of their idea of prophecy is pagan:
"You know that when you were gentiles you were led astray
to mute idols, however you may have been moved." It is this
kind of ecstatic speech, characteristic of Bacchanalian rites
among others, which has infiltrated the Corinthian church.
Paul does not reject it, but tries to place it in its proper setting. After all, he himself can speak ecstatically more than
any of them (14:18).

In his letter to the Romans, Paul lists various spiritual gifts
given to members of the church (12:6-8); the first of these
is prophecy, given to be used "in proportion to our faith"
(RSV). Paul does not criticize prophecy any more than he
does in 1 Corinthians. And since in regard to the Roman
community he knows of no difficulties produced by it, he
does not mention any qualifications except that of "proportion to our faith." It would appear that he expected some
Roman Christians to have an abundance of the prophetic
gift, just as others might be able to serve, teach, exhort, con-
tribute, govern, and give alms. This does not mean that there
is any "prophetic ministry" at Rome.

The situation is different, however, in the letter to the
Ephesians, where Paul speaks of the work of the ministry as
distributed by Christ among apostles, prophets, evangelists,
pastors, and teachers (4:11), and says that the Church is
built on the foundation of the apostles and prophets (2:20),
to whom the mystery of God's plan has been revealed by the
Spirit (3:5). If there is an office held by apostles, it presumably follows that there is an office held by prophets. This,
then, represents a continuation of the Corinthian situation,
where all can be encouraged to be zealous for prophesying
(14:39) but not all are prophets (12:29).

In the Acts of the Apostles, the church of Jerusalem receives power when the Holy Spirit comes upon it (1:8) at
Pentecost (2:1-4); this power includes the gift of prophecy
(2:17-18). It is not stated, however, that Jerusalem Christians became prophets. On the other hand, around the year

44 we do encounter Christian prophets at Jerusalem. One of them, named Agabus, comes to Antioch and predicts a universal famine (11:27-28). A little later we hear of "prophets and teachers" at Antioch; they include Barnabas (from Jerusalem), Symeon Niger, Lucius of Cyrene, Manaen, a member of the court of Herod the tetrarch, and Saul (13:1). Unfortunately, it is by no means clear whether "prophet" and "teacher" are mutually exclusive titles, and which persons held which offices. At the apostolic council in Jerusalem the decree is sent by apostles and elders, who also choose and send two men, Judas and Silas, who happen to be prophets (15:25, 32). Paul chooses Silas to go with him on a missionary journey (15:40) in accordance with the instructions of the Jerusalem church. Later Paul gives commands to Silas (17:15); but Silas apparently stays in Corinth after Paul leaves. Prophecy is mentioned in Acts at only one other place, Caesarea, where we encounter the unmarried daughters of the evangelist Philip (6:5), who prophesy (21:9), and the Jerusalem prophet Agabus, who predicts Paul's arrest (21:10-11).

It is evident that on the basis of these notices little can be said of any "prophetic ministry" in the Church. There are some prophets, chiefly members of the church of Jerusalem and subject to the apostles there. Their function is certainly not criticism of the hierarchy, but (for the most part) prediction.

Something like the "regularization" of prophecy appears in the Pastoral Epistles, where we learn that Timothy, like others, was not to disregard the gift of grace in himself, given to him "through prophecy" with the imposition of hands by the presbytery (1 Tim. 4:14). It would appear that the function of such prophecy was to indicate appropriate candidates for the ministry (1:18). Nothing in the Pastoral Epistles suggests that ecstatic speech was encouraged or, indeed, permitted. The only "prophet" mentioned is the ancient Greek poet Epimenides (Tit. 1:12).

D.   The Ministry in the Apostolic Fathers

When we turn from the New Testament to look at the
nature of the Christian ministry in the writings of the Apostolic Fathers, the first aspect of it that impresses us is its
unity within diversity. In the various writings we encounter
divers orders of ministers; but the range of the diversity is
not very great. The fact that it is not very great suggests that
the kinds of ministers there are come from the life of the
apostolic Church. There was room for selectivity but not for
absolutely free creativity. The widest diversity occurs in the
Didache, where we read of teachers, prophets, apostles, bishops, and deacons—all of them already mentioned in the New
Testament writings. At the same time, the diversity is beginning to be reduced. Those to whom the Didachist writes are
to appoint bishops and deacons whose ministry will be either
equivalent or analogous to that of the prophets and teachers.
We can say, then, that the primary ministry in the Didache
is that of apostles, prophets, and teachers; and that prophets
and teachers are beginning to be replaced by bishops and
deacons. In other writings of the Apostolic Fathers there are
other, but similar, kinds of ministries. In 1 Clement there
were, but no longer are, apostles; there are the successors of
the apostles, who are bishops and deacons (42:4-5), and the
presbyters, at least some of whom are equivalent to bishops
(cf. 54:2). For Ignatius there were the apostles who were
sent by Christ, and there are now bishops, presbyters (joined
in a "presbytery"), and deacons. Similarly Polycarp—as
bishop—writes a letter with his presbyters and refers to the
presbyters and deacons who minister among those to whom
he writes. Barnabas, as a teacher, refers only to teachers and
teaching. Finally, Hermas speaks of earlier apostles but, for
his own times, mentions only bishops, presbyters, teachers,
and (perhaps) deacons. The "prophets" whom he mentions
do not seem to hold any special ministerial office.

If we begin with the apostles, we see that they are essentially men of the past, men who provided models for later ministers or, as in 1 Clement, brought the ministry into existence in an apostolic succession from Christ and ultimately from God (chs. 42–44). The exception to this rule is provided in the Didache, where we read of itinerant apostles for whom regulations have to be set down (11:4-6). Like true teachers (11:1; cf. 4:1), they are to be received as the Lord, for—as in Matthew 10:40—he who receives them receives the Lord. They are not to stay anywhere more than two days, and they are to accept nothing but bread and lodging. Those who ask for money are false prophets. These instructions seem to be based on something like those given the Twelve in Matthew 10:6-42. They suggest either that the Didache was written when itinerant apostles were still making their journeys or that its author was looking back to the apostolic age. It can hardly be claimed that they prove the existence of itinerant apostles at a later time, for there is no other evidence to suggest that such was the case. It is possible, of course, that the word "apostle" was used in a very broad and inclusive sense; but evidence for this possibility, outside the Didache, is lacking. Indeed, the Didache goes on to indicate that the instructions about the "apostles" really apply to any itinerant Christians, for in chapter 12 it is stated that no traveling Christians are to remain more than three days; if they are craftsmen and wish to settle in the community, they are to work at their craft.

It would appear that in the Didache the real successors of the apostles are the prophets and the teachers. The prophets are allowed to say the Eucharistic prayer as they will (10:7) and they are not to be tested except in relation to their conduct (11:7-12). Both prophets and teachers, if they take up residence in the community, are to be regarded as workmen worthy of their food (as is said of the apostles in Matthew 10:10). Indeed, the status of the resident prophets is equivalent to that of the high priests in the Old Testament; they are to receive the "first fruits" of wine, grain, oxen, and sheep

(13:3), as well as of jars of wine or oil, money, clothing—and of all possessions (13:6-7). The priestly role of the resident prophet is significant not only in relation to the Judaism out of which it obviously emerged but also in relation to later Christian ideas about the ministry, as we shall see; for the ministry of the prophet leads toward the ministry of the bishop (15:1-2). Similarly, the role of the teacher is exalted in the Didache. He is the one who sets forth the "Way of the teaching" as described in chapters 1–6, as well as the liturgical instructions provided in chapters 7–10.

In the Didache, then, we find mention of "first apostles, second prophets, third teachers," just as in Paul's First Letter to the Corinthians (12:28). Very gradually, two other Pauline orders, bishops and deacons (Phil. 1:1), are being introduced. There is no mention of presbyters.

It could be, and has been, argued that the Didache sets forth the way in which the Christian ministry universally developed and that "charismatic" prophets were gradually supplanted everywhere by appointive bishops. We do not know, however, that such was the case. It sems more likely that in some communities this happened, while in other communities other changes took place.

If we look at 1 Clement, for example, we find no teachers and only Old Testament prophets (17:1; 43:1). The apostles were men of Clement's generation (5:1) but lived well before his own time. They are historical, not contemporary, personages. Clement says practically nothing of deacons (42:4-5), for they are apparently not involved in the controversy which concerns him. On the other hand, he insists that the apostles appointed their "first fruits" (a Pauline term, 1 Cor. 16:15) to be bishops and deacons of future believers (42:4). In turn, they provided for a succession of other men who were to be set over Christ's sheepfold. These men were called "presbyters" (44:5; 47:6; 54:2; 57:1) and their office was called "overseeing" or "episcopate" (44:1, 4) or, more generally, "ministry" (chs. 40, 41, and 44). Clement once refers to Christian "rulers" (1:3) but elsewhere he uses the word in reference to authorities Roman, Jewish, and pagan.

We do not know how Clement knew what he tells us about the apostles' appointment of the first bishops and deacons. His language in chapter 42 recalls that of Acts (1:3, 2:4, 14:23) and of two Pauline epistles (1 Cor. 16:15; Phil. 1:1); perhaps he is relying on the New Testament. On the other hand, it is quite possible that tradition before him had shaped the story in the form in which he tells it. In chapter 44, however, we may wonder if he does not rely on Acts, specifically the account of Paul's farewell to the Ephesian presbyters at Miletus (20:17-38). In that account occurs the formula, "remembering the words of the Lord Jesus" (20:35), which Clement uses twice (13:1; 46:7). In it we find the presbyters described as set over the sheepfold as bishops (20:28)—and this correlation of presbyters with bishops is characteristic of Clement's thought. We must conclude that he either knows Acts or is influenced by a kind of thought very close to that of Luke. He explicitly states that the presbyters are set over the sheepfold (54:2).

Conceivably, not all presbyters are bishops, and not all bishops are presbyters; but Clement does not say so. Instead, he states that Christians are to serve God, each in his own rank, and are not to transgress the appointed rule (kanōn) of their service (41:1). What is this rule? He has previously compared the Church to any army in which various officers, each in his own rank (again!), carry out the commands of their superiors (36:3). More important, he has insisted upon the importance of the parallel provided by the ministries of the high priest, the priests, and the Levites in Judaism (40:5). The parallel is made especially clear when we compare the "offerings" performed by the high priest or under his guidance (40:2, 4; 41:2) with the offering of gifts by those who hold the office of the episcopate (44:4).

It seems hard to deny that for Clement the episcopate is

analogous to the office of the high priest. But if this is so, we should expect to find presbyters the equivalent of priests, and deacons the equivalent of Levites; and such precise equivalences are certainly not to be found in the letter.

It is difficult to tell exactly what has happened at Corinth. It seems possible, however, that the situation involved a presbyter-bishop who achieved some sort of primacy only by deposing other presbyter-bishops. Clement gives the example of Moses, who "asks forgiveness for the people or begs that he himself may be blotted out together with them" (53:5) and then urges some leader to be "noble, compassionate, filled with love" and to accept voluntary exile—perhaps at Rome—for the sake of the community (ch. 54); he also provides parallels from kings and rulers among the gentiles (55:1). The solution for the difficulty is to be found in renewed obedience to the presbyters (57:1). "It is better for you to be found small but honorable in the sheepfold of Christ than to seem pre-eminent but be cast out from his hope" (57:2).

If such a hypothesis were to be viewed as tenable, we might suggest that the reason Clement does not refer more precisely to the high-priestly office of the bishop is that he does not want the present Corinthian bishop to continue as high priest. Indeed, the Corinthian troubles will come to an end only if this bishop withdraws and lets the other presbyter-bishops govern the community.

Perhaps one can venture to say this much about the church of Corinth; from Clement's letter we learn nothing directly about the organization of the church of Rome. He writes in the name of the whole Church and says nothing about the Roman situation—except what we can learn from his general remarks about the origin of the Christian ministry. These remarks show that at Rome there were bishops (probably presbyter-bishops) and deacons. Further details are lacking.

If we compare 1 Clement with the Didache, we find similarities in titles but remarkable dissimilarities in functions.

As we have pointed out, in the Didache the prophets and the teachers are pre-eminent, though they are about to be supplanted by bishops and deacons. In 1 Clement the presbyter-bishops and the deacons are pre-eminent, and there are no prophets or teachers. There is not the slightest hint that there ever were prophets and teachers. Therefore, we conclude, the ministry at Rome and the ministry in the area from which the Didache comes were quite different in origin, though something like the early Roman ministry is envisaged toward the end of the Didache.

At this point we should turn to the Shepherd of Hermas in order to see what the ministry at Rome was like some decades after Clement wrote. Here too the apostles are men of the past, and in the Ninth Similitude they are almost invariably associated with teachers also dead (15, 4; 16, 5; 25, 2). A period of transition is explicitly mentioned in the Third Vision (5, 1), where stones in the tower which is the Church are identified as apostles, bishops, teachers, and deacons; some of these have fallen asleep and some are still alive. In general, we should assume, the apostles and teachers are dead while the bishops and deacons are alive. Of the bishops we learn little, except that they, or some of them, are hospitable and help the destitute and the widows of the community (Sim. 9, 27, 2). It is not clear whether or not anything specific is said about the deacons; those called *diakonoi* who have robbed widows and orphans and made gain from their ministry may be "ministers" in general (Sim. 9, 26, 2).

We know, therefore, that there are bishops and deacons; but we know little about them. On the other hand, there is a key passage (Vis. 2, 4, 3) in which Hermas explicitly speaks of "the elders who are in charge of the church." This must show that bishops and presbyters, as in Clement's letter, are practically identical; it also suggests that no one presbyter was to be called *the* bishop.

In addition, there are false prophets who deal with coteries and true prophets who speak, inspired by the Spirit, during liturgical worship (Mand. 11); it cannot be said, however, that the prophet has a special office. Instead, he has a special function—but anyone through whom the Spirit works can exercise it.[11] The situation reflected in Clement and that reflected in Hermas are therefore essentially the same.

Less significant information about the ministry is provided in 2 Clement, where we see that the apostles (14:2), apparently including Peter (5:3-4), are known primarily from writings. The presbyters give exhortations in liturgical worship (17:3)—after a reading from scripture (19:1)—and are to be obeyed (17:5). Nothing is said of bishops or of any other ministers. Barnabas tells us even less. Once more, the apostles are historical figures (5:9). Barnabas himself, though he modestly denies the fact (1:8; 4:9), is obviously a teacher who has the spiritual gift of (private?) teaching (9:8).

We now turn to the person who says most about the ministry among the Apostolic Fathers, the one whose ideas at a later time were by far the most influential. This is Ignatius, bishop of Antioch or, indeed, of all Syria (Rom. 2:2).

For Ignatius the apostles are men of the past, like Peter and Paul (Rom. 4:3). They are men through whom the Lord worked (Magn. 7:1) and they gave decrees still binding upon Christians (cf. Trall. 7:1, 13:2). Ignatius himself does not venture to give commands as if he were an apostle (Trall. 3:3; Rom. 4:3; cf. Eph. 3:1). In the story of salvation they are joined with the patriarchs and prophets of the Old Testament (Philad. 9:1); they were subject to the Christ and the Father (Magn. 13:2). For the Church of Ignatius' time they had been replaced by the presbyters (Magn. 6:1; Trall. 2:2, 3:1; Philad. 5:1; Smyrn. 8:1) and, as we shall see, by the bishops.

For Ignatius the ministry consists not only of presbyters but also of bishops and deacons, all appointed by the purpose of Jesus Christ and established by him, by his Holy Spirit

[11] The prophets mentioned in Sim. 9, 15, 4 are Old Testament prophets.

(Philad. inscr.). The only prophets he knows are Old Testament prophets; the only teacher is Jesus Christ (Eph. 15:1; Magn. 9:1). Although, or because, such ministers as prophets and teachers are lacking, Ignatius can express his views of a threefold ministry with considerable clarity. Usually, but not always, he compares the bishop to God; the presbyters to the apostles; and the deacons to Jesus Christ. Yet this hierarchical arrangement lacks symmetry. We should expect the sequence bishop-God, presbyters-Christ, and deacons-apostles. Since what we would expect is not what there is, we may perhaps infer that Ignatius' scheme is a combination of two elements: in one there were bishops and deacons, compared to God and Christ; in the other, presbyters compared with, or taking the place of, apostles. Conceivably we can infer that the ministry of bishops and deacons is that mentioned in the Didache, while that of presbyters is that mentioned in Acts. Actually, however, we are not in a position to trace the literary origins of the notions.

More important are the sources of the ideas involved. For Ignatius bishops are a "type" or copy of God (Trall. 3:1), who can be called the bishop of all (Magn. 3:1). But the bishop can also be compared with Jesus Christ (Trall. 2:1; Rom. 9:1); and it is clear that he also has a role co-ordinate with that which the apostles possessed.

> Everyone whom the master of the house sends to do his business, we ought to receive as him who sent him. So it is evident that we must regard the bishop as the Lord himself (Eph. 6:1).

The "master of the house" may be derived from the parable in Matthew (21:33) and following (he is evidently identified with God himself), while the words "receive as him who sent him" recall a saying of Jesus recorded in Matthew 10:40 and John 13:20.

Matthew	*John*
He who receives you receives me, and he who receives me receives him who sent me.	He who receives whomever I send receives me, and he who receives me receives him who sent me.

The bishop, sent by the Lord, is therefore to be received as the Lord (cf. Didache 11:2, 4); and he is thus analogous to the apostle.

It would appear that Ignatius' idea of the relationship between Christians and their bishop, as based upon the relationship between Jesus and the Father, is derived from an interpretation of the Gospel of John. (1) As Jesus is united with the Father, and the apostles are united with Jesus, so the Church must be united with the bishop and presbyters (Magn. 7:1; Eph. 5:1; in part repeated in Smyrn. 8:2). Such a picture is clearly Johannine in origin; compare John 17:23: "I in them and thou in me." (2) As Jesus was sent by the Father (Magn. 8:2; he also "came forth" from the Father, Magn. 7), and the apostles were sent by the Lord, so the bishop has been sent (Eph. 6:1). This too is Johannine: the Father sent Jesus and Jesus sent the disciples (John 13:20, 17:18, 20:21, etc.), and Jesus came from the Father (8:42, 13:3, 16:27, etc.). (3) As Jesus follows the Father—and the apostles follow Jesus, though Ignatius does not explicitly say so—so the Church follows the bishop (Smyrn. 8:1, Magn. 7). (4) As Jesus is subject to the Father, so the Church is subject to the bishop (Magn. 13:2; cf. Trall. 2:1). Both these ideas, of following and of being subject, are paralleled in John (5:19, 30; 8:28-29; 10:30). (5) Finally, "he who honors the bishop has been honored by God" (Smyrn. 9:1), for to honor the bishop is to honor the Son, and to honor the Son is to honor the Father (John 5:23), and "if anyone serves me, the Father will honor him" (John 12:26).

Because the bishop takes the place of the earlier apostle, Ignatius not only can use the language of the Gospels about apostles and apply it to the bishop, as we have seen (Eph.

6:1), but also can use what Paul said of himself and apply it to the bishop of Philadelphia (Philad. 1:1):"I know that your bishop obtained the ministry, which makes for common benefit, not 'from himself or through men' " (Gal. 1:1). There is a structure not only hierarchical but also historical which evidently begins with God and proceeds through Christ to the apostles, the bishops (other ministers subordinate to them), and the Church.

New Testament teaching does not fully explain how Ignatius could move from the apostles to the bishops, for the bishop is mentioned in the singular only three times (1 Tim. 3:2; Tit. 1:7; 1 Pet. 2:25—of Christ, cf. Ignatius, Rom. 9:1) and in the plural only twice (Acts 20:28; Phil. 1:1). Perhaps the link between the New Testament and Ignatius lies in the Jewish-American idea of the principal ministers as high priests. We have already observed that such language is used in the Didache and in 1 Clement. It may be added that in second-century Christianity the apostles James and John were regarded as having been high priests.[12] And in contemporary Judaism the high priest was viewed both as the center of unity for the community and as the representative of God (Josephus, *Contra Apionem* 2, 193–194).

We venture to suppose, then, that Ignatius has relied upon Christian traditions prior to himself and has developed their implications in creating his portrait of the bishops' office. He explicitly says that Jesus is "the high priest who has been entrusted with Holy of Holies, who alone has been entrusted with the secret things of God" (Philad. 9:1). The bishop, to be received as the Lord, has an office like the Lord's. Just so, Clement of Rome, who certainly regards Jesus as the great high priest (36:1; 61:3; 64), seems also to treat the chief ministers as at least analogous to high priests.[13]

[12] Epiphanius, *Pan.* 29, 4, 4; Eusebius, *H.E.* 5, 24, 3.
[13] The fact that Ignatius mentions no Roman bishop proves nothing; in his letter to the Romans he does not mention either presbyters or deacons, and in his view (1) there is no church without a bishop (Trall. 3:1) and (2) bishops have been appointed throughout the world (Eph. 3:2).

Bishops, however, are not the only ministers of whom Ignatius speaks, nor do they exercise the only "ministry" (*diakonia*) he knows. Indeed, he mentions the bishop's ministry only once (Philad. 1:1), that of the deacon three times (Magn. 6:1; Philad. 10:2; Smyrn. 12:2). Individual deacons are mentioned four times, thrice by name (Eph. 2:1; Magn. 2:1; Philad. 11:1) and once with reference to the appointment of one to go to Antioch (Philad. 10:1). Far more often (fourteen times) Ignatius speaks of deacons collectively. They are obviously lower in rank than the other ministers; he says that the deacon Zotion is subject to the bishop as to the grace of God and to the presbytery as to the law of Jesus Christ (Magn. 2); and although he once speaks of the bishop and presbyters without mentioning deacons (Magn. 7:1), he never speaks of deacons without mentioning other orders —except in one instance where he refers to a deacon who is serving him (Philad. 11:1). The deacons have been trusted with the service of Jesus Christ (Magn. 6:1); more specifically, they are "deacons of the mysteries of Jesus Christ"— not "deacons of food and drink but servants of the Church of God" who "must please all in every way" (Trall. 2:3). Behind Ignatius' language lie two passages in which the apostle Paul speaks of his own ministry. The first is 1 Corinthians 4:1, where he refers to apostles as "servants of Christ and stewards of the mysteries of God"; the second is 1 Corinthians 10:33, where he says that he pleases all in every way. Obviously the office of the deacon is viewed as a continuation of the office of the apostle. The mention of food and drink suggests that the deacons take part in the Eucharistic distribution; Ignatius may have in mind something like the story of the archetypal deacons in Acts 6:1-6.[14]

Presbyters are mentioned nine times, always in the plural, though two individuals are named in Magnesians 2. They take the place of what Ignatius calls the "sanhedrin of the

[14] And when he speaks of deacons as his "fellow slaves," he is probably thinking of Col. 1:7.

apostles" (Magn. 6:1) and constitute a "sanhedrin of God" (Trall. 3:1); thus they correspond to the Jewish sanhedrin which gave counsel to the high priest.[15] The "holy presbyters" of Magnesia do not take advantage of their bishop's outwardly youthful appearance but yield to him as prudent in God (Magn. 3:1). Ignatius calls upon the Trallian presbyters to "refresh" the bishop (Trall. 12:2). His view of presbyters as a collective group is made clear by his frequent use (thirteen times) of the word "presbytery." The Ephesian presbytery is attuned to the bishop as the strings to a lyre (Eph. 4:1); the Magnesian presbytery is the "worthily woven spiritual crown" of the church (Magn. 13:1). The presbyters, like the bishop and deacons, "have been appointed by the plan of Jesus Christ," who "established them in security in accordance with his will by his Holy Spirit" (Philad. inscr.).

The functions of the presbyters are not altogether clear, for it is the bishop who leads the prayer of the church (Eph. 5:2), celebrates the Eucharist, and conducts baptisms and common meals (Smyrn. 8:1-2), gives counsel on matters of spiritual discipline, and permits marriages to take place (Polyc. 5:2-3); he also gives homilies on various subjects (5:1). He convokes the councils of the church (7:2). Apparently, however, the presbyter can celebrate the Eucharist if he is appointed by the bishop to do so (Smyrn. 8:1).

From Ignatius' letter to Polycarp we know that Polycarp was aware of this kind of ministerial doctrine.[16] It is sometimes claimed, however, that the bishop of Smyrna was not really committed to a high episcopal order, and that when he began his letter to the Philippians with the words "Polycarp and the presbyters with him," he really meant "Polycarp and the presbyters who are on his side," and was not speaking "ex cathedra" as a bishop. It is true that Polycarp does not mention bishops in his letter, though it is concerned with

[15] Perhaps Ignatius refers to the unity of the presbyters when he speaks of "the sanhedrin of the bishop" (Philad. 8:1), but this is uncertain.
[16] It should also be recalled that Polycarp collected the Ignatian letters.

matters of order. Perhaps, however, this omission does not prove that there was no bishop at Philippi; after all, bishops are mentioned in Paul's letter to the Philippians.

He describes the qualifications of deacons in a way strikingly reminiscent of a similar description in 1 Timothy 3:8-13 and urges the congregation to be subject to the presbyters and the deacons as to God and Christ (5:2-3). What Ignatius says of the deacons' status (Trall. 3:1) thus remains unaltered; but Polycarp applies to the presbyters what Ignatius says of the bishop. As for these presbyters, their qualifications (6:1) are set forth in a list not very different from the one concerning deacons. The most important passage about a presbyter, however, is chapter 11, about a certain Valens, "formerly made a presbyter among you." He and his wife have apparently been excommunicated, but Polycarp urges the church to call them back if they repent. Of his avarice Polycarp writes, "How can one who does not control himself in such matters make pronouncements to another?" This question is raised in 1 Timothy 3:5—in regard to the bishop. Is it not possible to infer that the reason for Polycarp's silence about bishops lies in the episcopal office of the deposed Valens?

The three writers who most clearly advocate a "regular" ministry say nothing about contemporary prophets or prophecy. For Clement, Ignatius, and Polycarp (not to mention Barnabas) the only prophets are those of the Old Testament. What has become of the prophet's function? Only one clue is given us, and this is to be found in Ignatius' account of his visit to Philadelphia (7:1-2). The Spirit came to him and inspired him so that he cried out "with a loud voice, the voice of God"; it was the Spirit which was making a proclamation—about the necessity of heeding the regular ministers of the Church. This is to say that if there is any prophecy in the churches which Ignatius knows, it is expressed in the channels of church order.

Later in the second century there were archaizing prophetic movements, primarily in Montanism and secondarily among Gnostics, but it was generally believed that the order achieved in Ignatius' time deserved preference. Whether we treat this order as the result of a development or as the expression of the decay of spiritual power, it did become established in the second century.

The role of the teacher too was taken over by the regular ministers. Neither Clement nor Polycarp mentions teachers, and Ignatius knows only one: Jesus Christ (Eph. 15:1; Magn. 9:2). As a special office, that of teaching survived, and only for a time, in Jewish Christianity, where we meet it in the Didache, in Barnabas, and in Hermas. Papias too viewed the Church as like a school, for he asked what the elders, disciples of their teachers (the apostles), had learned from them.

The lack of emphasis on teaching is clear enough from the ways in which Clement uses the verb "to teach." The Lord Jesus taught gentleness and patience (13:1); Paul taught the whole world righteousness (5:7); and the Corinthians formerly taught the duties of the ideal housewife (1:3).

IV.   Liturgy in the Apostolic Fathers

One of the most important aspects of the continuity of the Apostolic Fathers with the rest of early Christianity lies in their reference to liturgical matters. First, the writings of the Apostolic Fathers contain references to the liturgical worship of the early communities. The Didache includes directions for baptism and the Eucharist; 1 Clement concludes with an extended prayer; 2 Clement is a homily read in a liturgical context; Ignatius often discusses the Eucharist; and Eucharistic prayers are to be found in the Martyrdom of Polycarp. Second, the writings of the Apostolic Fathers were employed in the prayers of the Church at later dates, from the third century to the fifth. In various prayers, chiefly Eucharistic, we find echoes of the Didache, Clement, and

Ignatius. This is to say that the Apostolic Fathers reflect the prayer of the Church in their time and earlier, while they influence the prayer as it comes to be expressed later. They stand between the Apostolic Age and the age of the great theologians and councils.

Before we discuss the liturgy as such, we should briefly mention the evidence of the Apostolic Fathers as to the day on which it was usually performed.

A. Sunday

Without the evidence of the Apostolic Fathers it would be impossible to determine absolutely the day on which early Christians celebrated their principal rites. To be sure, one might infer that since the resurrection appearances in the Gospels took place on the first day of the week (Sunday), this was the day of worship. Furthermore, Christians at Troas met on the first day "to break bread" (Acts 20:7), but this could conceivably be regarded as unusual, like John's being "in the Spirit on the Lord's day" (Rev. 1:10).[17] From the Didache, Barnabas, and Ignatius, however, we learn of the importance of Sunday.

According to the Didache (14:1) Christians are to meet "on the Lord's day of the Lord" (*kata kyriaken de kyriou*) in order to break bread and offer thanksgiving. The theological significance of the day is pointed out by Barnabas. "The present Sabbaths are not acceptable to me, but the one which I made, when after resting from everything I will make the beginning of the eighth day—which is the beginning of another world." After these words ascribed to God Barnabas continues, "For this reason we keep the eighth day with gladness, when also Jesus rose from the dead and after being made manifest ascended into the heavens" (15:8-9). Similarly, Ignatius, arguing with Judaizers, claims that the Old Testament prophets "no longer observed the Sabbath but lived in relation to the Lord's (day), when also our life ap-

[17] The first day of 1 Cor. 16:2 has no necessary connection with worship.

peared through him and his death" (Magn. 9:1). His idea
of the prophets' rejection of the Sabbath is presumably based
on Isaiah 1:13; and that he has Sunday in mind is clear from
his use of the verb *aneteilen* (appeared), ordinarily employed
of sunrise.

The picture is made only more explicit when Justin says
(*Apol.* 1, 67):

> On what is called Sunday there is an assembly of all these
> who live in city or country. . . . We all share in the assembly
> on Sunday, since it is the first day, when God made darkness
> and matter firm and made the universe, and Jesus Christ our
> Saviour on the same day rose from the dead; for on the day
> before Saturday they crucified him and on the day after
> Saturday—i.e., Sunday—he appeared to his apostles and dis-
> ciples and taught these things.

B. Liturgical Matters

The most important document for liturgical study is obviously the Didache, which explicitly deals with baptism, fasting, prayers, and Eucharist (7–10:4).

The Didachist states that baptism, following the recitation
of the catechism (chs. 1–6), is to be in the name of the
Father, and the Son, and the Holy Spirit, and in cold running
water, if possible. If water for immersion is not available, a
smaller amount may be poured three times on the candidate's
head. Fasting, for as long as a day or two, is to precede the
baptism. These directions agree with much of what we know
from somewhat later writers. Justin (*Apol.* 1, 61, 2-3) describes the prebaptismal catechism and fasting and the use
of the threefold name. Tertullian states that the kind of water
used is not all-important (*Bapt.* 4, 3) and mentions the fast
(20). Cyprian (*Ep.* 69, 12-14) refers to affusion. The length
of the prebaptismal fast agrees with what we find in the
Clementine Recognitions (7, 37; 10, 72). This is to say either
that Christian practice was generally fairly uniform or that
Jewish-Christian practice was almost normative.

The Didachist also says that fasting is not to occur on the days used by Jews—Mondays and Thursdays—but on Wednesdays and Fridays. The fact of Wednesday/Friday fasting is attested by Clement (*Str.* 7, 75, 2) and Tertullian (*Ieiun.* 14) more than a century later, but it may also be reflected in Hermas' mention of a "station" (Sim. 5:1).

As for praying, the Lord's Prayer is to be used—three times a day. Similarly, Clement (*Str.* 7, 40, 3-4) and Tertullian (*Orat.* 25; *Ieiun.* 10) speak of the hours of prayer as the third, sixth, and ninth.

The Eucharistic prayers of the Didache (chs. 9–10), as Dibelius demonstrated, are essentially based on Jewish table prayers, though they have clearly been made Christian.

> We give thee thanks, our Father,
>> For the holy Vine of thy child David
>>> which thou didst make known to us through thy child Jesus:
>>>> to thee be glory forever. (Amen).

> We give thee thanks, our Father
>> for the life and knowledge
>>> which thou didst make known to us through thy child Jesus:
>>>> to thee be glory forever. (Amen).

> As this broken bread was scattered upon the mountains
>> but was brought together and became one,
> So let thy Church be brought together from the ends of the earth
>> into thy kingdom:
> For thine is the glory and the power through
>> Jesus Christ
>> forever. (Amen).

> We give thee thanks, holy Father,
>> for thy holy name,
>>> which thou didst tabernacle in our hearts, and
>> for the knowledge and faith and immortality
>>> which thou didst make known to us through thy child Jesus:
>>>> to thee be glory forever. (Amen).

> Thou, Lord, didst create all things and didst for thy name's sake,
>> give food and drink to men for their enjoyment,
>> that they might give thanks to thee; but thou

> hast blessed us with spiritual food and drink,
>   and eternal life through thy child.
> Above all we give thee thanks
>   because thou art mighty.
>   To thee be glory forever. (Amen).
>
> Remember, Lord, thy Church,
>   to deliver it from every evil and
>   to perfect it in thy love, and
>
> bring it together from the four winds,
>   sanctified,
>   into thy kingdom, which thou hast prepared for it;
> For thine is the power and the glory forever. (Amen).
>
> Let grace come and let this world pass away.
>
> Hosanna to the God of David.
>
> If anyone is holy, let him come;
> if anyone is not, let him repent;
> *Marana tha*; Amen.

Important and striking parallels connect this prayer, or these prayers, not only with Jewish prototypes but also with the theological ideas reflected in John 16–17 and in other Christian literature. In other words, the Didache does not reflect simply a Christianized Judaism; it is fully Christian as well as Jewish.

In 1 Clement we hear more about Jewish liturgy than we do about Christian. The sacrifices offered by the high priest and other ministers are rather fully discussed (chs. 40–41) but then nothing is said about the Christian Eucharist, and van Unnik has shown that the Sanctus cannot be located in the Eucharist simply on the basis of what Clement says in ch. 34.[18] On the other hand, Clement is certainly a witness to the common use of doxologies, for they occur in 20:12, 32:4, 38:4, 45:7-8, 50:7, 58:2, 61:3, 64, and 65:2. Toward the end of the letter there is a prayer (59:3–61:3) which has been compared both with Eucharistic prayers of the Roman

[18] *Vigiliae Christianae* 5 (1951), 204-248.

church and with magical papyri—with the first to show that here we have a "normative" Roman prayer, with the second to show how well it fits into its cultural environment. Actually the prayer contains many of the themes developed earlier in the letter, and one may suppose that Clement was capable of praying without following a fixed model.

From the homily known as 2 Clement we learn that sermons were sometimes read, not memorized, and that the reader may have held a special office—but this is uncertain (19:1).

Ignatius tells us something about baptism and the Eucharist, but not a great deal with explicit detail. One might suppose that a liturgical papyrus of the fifth century, in which we find the Ignatian terms "drug of immortality" and "antidote to death," could show that Ignatius took the terms from a liturgy. This was what Lietzmann, who first discussed the papyrus, originally thought; and he was followed by H. W. Bartsch.[19] Lietzmann's ground for this notion was extraordinarily flimsy. Liturgies, he wrote in 1926, are not accustomed to contain quotations from church fathers. Therefore Ignatius used some liturgy and was not quoted in one. The next year, however, Lietzmann published the papyrus and changed his mind. He had discovered meanwhile that in Greek liturgies there are actual quotations from Pseudo-Dionysius and from 1 Clement.[20] The new facts made the old theory inadequate. All we can say is that Ignatius used the kind of language which several centuries later was to appear suitable for liturgical expression.

Ignatius mentions baptism several times. It is obviously a rite of great significance, for it can be described as the equivalent of arms for use in the struggle against hostile powers (Polyc. 6:2; cf. Eph. 13:1). Jesus himself was baptized, both "so that all righteousness might be fulfilled by him" (Smyr.

[19] *Gnostisches Gut und Gemeindetradition bei Ignatius von Antiochien* (Gütersloh, 1940), 113.

[20] "Ein liturgischer Papyrus des Berliner Museum," *Festgabe für Adolf Julicher* (Tübingen, 1927), 213-228.

1:1; Matt. 3:15), and "so that by the passion he might purify the water" (Eph. 18:2). Since Ignatius obviously regards the Lord's actions as providing a model for Christians to follow, it is significant that in one account of the baptism he mentions first anointing and then baptism—a sequence later found among Syrian Christians. Christians who are baptized, one would assume, also fulfill all righteousness. And when Ignatius says that the baptism was closely related to the passion, we are reminded of the strong statement in 1 John 5:6 that Jesus Christ came through water and blood—not by water only but by water and blood.

The Eucharist occupies his attention more fully, largely because it is a matter of controversy: heretics abstain from it, as from worship in general, because they do not acknowledge the Eucharist to be the flesh of Jesus Christ (Smyrn. 7:1). The same notion seems to be implied in Philad. 4: "Use one Eucharist, for one is the flesh of our Lord Jesus Christ. . . ." Here Ignatius adds that one is the cup for uniting with his blood, one sanctuary, as there is one bishop. The emphasis upon Eucharistic unity strongly resembles that expressed by Paul in 1 Corinthians 10:16-17.

The Eucharist is important because the flesh of Jesus suffered for our sins and was raised by the Father (Smyrn. 7:1); union with his flesh and blood, as in Johannine thought, produces salvation. His flesh is "the bread of God"; his blood is "imperishable love" (Rom. 7:3). Therefore Ignatius can refer to "breaking the one loaf" (1 Cor. 10:16-17) and can identify it as "the drug of immortality, the antidote to dying" (Eph. 20:2). The notion that such expressions were common in mystery religions has never been confirmed by evidence; presumably Ignatius is making use of imaginative rhetoric in order to convey his thought. The thought itself seems to be primarily Pauline-Johannine.

The Eucharist, like baptism and the "agape" (whether separate from the Eucharist or not), is to be celebrated by the bishop or his delegate (Smyrn. 8:1-2). Indeed, the congregation is to follow the bishop's guidance in all cultic matters, including weddings (Polyc. 5:2).

Cultic matters in general are very significant for the life of the churches. Assemblies ought to take place as often as possible (Polyc. 4:2) because when Christians meet frequently the powers of Satan are destroyed and his destructiveness is dissolved in the harmony of Christian faith (Eph. 13:1). Similar recommendations of frequent meetings are to be found in Didache 16:2, 2 Clement 17:3, and (considerably later) Theophilus, *Ad Autolycum* 2, 38.

Ignatius urges his readers, in Paul's words (1 Thess. 5:17), to "pray without ceasing" (Eph. 10:1; Polyc. 1:3; cf. also Polycarp, Phil. 8:1). Their prayer is to be offered for others, not for themselves (Eph. 10:1); when they are cursed, they are to pray for their adversaries (Eph. 10:2; Smyrn. 4:1), as in the Gospel commandments (Matt. 5:44; Luke 6:28). The prayer is a united prayer of the church (Magn. 7:1), a mutual or reciprocal prayer (Trall. 12:2). The prayer of one or two is efficacious (Matt. 18:16-20), but that of the bishop and the whole church is much more efficacious (Eph. 5:2). Heretics abstain not only from the Eucharist but also from common prayer because they reject the reality of salvation (Smyrn. 7:1).

Ignatius uses the formula "remember in your prayers" (Magn. 14; Trall. 13:1) or "prayer" (Rom. 9:1), or simply "remember" (Eph. 21:1) when he is asking the churches to pray for him and/or the church in Syria. This formula occurs in all the letters from Smyrna, but not in those later sent from Troas—for by that time he could say that "your prayer reached the church at Antioch in Syria" (Smyrn. 11:1, 3; cf. Polyc. 7:1). What is constant in the letters of both periods is the expression of hope that by means of the prayer of the various churches he himself will attain salvation (Eph. 1:2; cf. 11:2, 20:1; Philad. 5:1, 8:2; Smyrn. 11:1). The "remembering" is clearly the community's remembering him before God.

In the Martyrdom of Polycarp 14 we find a prayer of thanksgiving which presumably is close to the prayers the bishop was accustomed to offer on liturgical occasions.

Lord God Almighty,
　　Father of thy beloved and blessed child Jesus Christ,
　　　through whom we obtain knowledge of thee,
　　God of angels and powers and of all creation,
　　　and of the race of the righteous who live in thy presence;

I bless thee
　　because thou hast judged me worthy of this day and hour,
　　　to take part in the number of the martyrs—
　　　　　in the cup of thy Christ
　　　　　　for the resurrection to eternal life of soul and body
　　　　　　in the imperishability of the Holy Spirit—
　　　among whom may I be expected in thy presence today,
　　　　　as a rich and acceptable sacrifice,
　　　　　as thou hast prepared and manifested and fulfilled it,
O God unlying and true.

Therefore for all things I praise thee,
　　　I bless thee,
　　　I glorify thee,
　　through the eternal and heavenly high priest Jesus Christ,
　　thy beloved child,
　　　　through whom to thee, with him and the Holy Spirit,
　　　　be glory both now and to the coming ages.
　　　　Amen.

The phraseology of this prayer recalls not only the prayers of the Didache but also the language of John ("resurrection to eternal life," John 5:29), of Polycarp himself (Christ the high priest, Phil. 12:2), and of later liturgical usage.[21] The passage "I praise thee, I bless thee, I glorify thee" resembles the Gloria in Excelsis.[22]

As we examine liturgical elements like these, we must constantly bear in mind the fact that although an individual bishop might well tend to pray in a rather stereotyped

[21] See J. A. Robinson in *Journal of Theological Studies* 21 (1919-20), 97-105; 24 (1922-23), 141-144; J. W. Tyrer, *ibid.* 23 (1921-22), 390-391; F. E. Brightman, *ibid.*, 391-392.
[22] See *Apostolic Constitutions* 7, 47, 2.

manner—especially, perhaps, a bishop as old as Polycarp was
—still there was considerable freedom of expression, provided that the primary concerns of the Church were set
forth in the prayer.

The Didache explicitly states (10:7) that prophets are to
say the Eucharistic prayer as they will; the prayer at the end
of 1 Clement recapitulates themes expressed earlier in the
letter and is therefore not based on a fixed form; and Justin
clearly shows that there was liturgical variety. This variety,
as R. P. C. Hanson has demonstrated, continued to exist in
the third century as well as the second. The liturgy was by
no means rigidly set. Modern slogans like "western usage"
were still meaningless.[23]

V.   Christian Life

The writings of the Apostolic Fathers, like those of the
New Testament authors, are rather disappointing to those
who look for social ethics in them. At the same time, the
proclamation of the kingdom of God, as set forth in the
synoptic Gospels, is maintained among the Fathers especially
influenced by Jewish Christianity. Admittedly, it is not very
prominent in 1 Clement (42:3, 50:3) or in the letters of
Ignatius (only in allusions to 1 Cor. 6:9, in Eph. 16:1 and in
Philad. 3:3) or in Polycarp (synoptic allusion in 2:3; 1 Cor.
6:9 in 5:3). But in 2 Clement, the Didache, Barnabas, and
Hermas it is more often mentioned.

In 2 Clement we hear of entering the kingdom of God by
means of mutual love (9:6) or righteous acts (11:7), though
Christians do not know the day when the kingdom will come
(12:1). It will actually come when "we speak with one
another in truth," when the soul expresses itself in good
works, and when thoughts of sex are transcended (12:3-5).

In the Didache the kingdom is mentioned only in prayers;

[23] "The Liberty of the Bishop to Improvise Prayer in the Eucharist,"
Vigiliae Christianae 15 (1961), 173-176.

in the Lord's Prayer (8:2) and in two prayers asking God to gather the Church from the ends of the earth into his kingdom (9:4, 10:5).

In the Shepherd of Hermas the kingdom is discussed only in relation to baptism and primarily with use of gospel passages (Sim. 9, 12–16, 20, 29). No one can enter the kingdom of God except by taking upon himself God's name, which is the name of his Son. He must also be clothed with twelve virtues and bear their names. He must receive the seal of the water of baptism (cf. John 3:5). The rich enter the kingdom with difficulty (Matt. 19:23); but those who are like newborn infants will live in the kingdom of God (Matt. 18:3).

It is obvious that among these writings the Didache expresses most clearly the eschatological idea of the kingdom; in 2 Clement the eschatology is present but is combined, as we have seen (Section I), with a strong emphasis on the importance of the Church; and in Hermas the kingdom is virtually identical with the Church. It may be that these differences can be explained as due to the development of Christian thought; it is more likely that they reflect local diversities, with the Didache representing ideas found in some Syrian community, 2 Clement and Hermas ideas expressed at Rome.

The closest these writers come to social ethics, it would appear, is in their discussions of the relationship of Christians to the state (see Chapter IV, Section I). Otherwise they are primarily concerned with the morality of individuals and small groups. Such a concern, involving a certain measure of self-centeredness, was inevitable in the circumstances under which early Christianity arose and in which it existed. The problems of society with which our age is so much preoccupied did not concern any of the early Christian writers, nor did they concern most of the Graeco-Roman philosophers or theologians with whom they might have come into contact. Indeed, the first writer to consider social problems with regard to Christianity was the anti-Christian writer Celsus, toward the end of the second century.[24]

We therefore turn to some of the more prominent statements about individual morality to be found in the Apostolic Fathers.

Especially in the more Jewish-oriented writings of the Apostolic Fathers there is a strong emphasis upon *practical beneficence*. Thus the Didache (1:5) urges the prospective Christian to give to everyone who asks (cf. Luke 6:30); the responsibility for determining whether the beneficiary is worthy or not is not the donor's but the beneficiary's; if he did not need what he received, he will have to "repay the last quadrans" (Matt. 5:26). To be sure, the last sentence of Didache 1 contradicts this statement: "Let your alms sweat in your hand until you know to whom you are giving" (apparently a quotation from Sirach). But the Didachist may wish to temper his enthusiasm for giving alms.

Other ideas recur from Sirach. "Do not be one who stretches out his hands to receive but shuts them when it comes to giving" (4:5; Sir. 4:36). "Do not turn away the needy but share everything with your brother, not calling it your own" (4:8; Sir. 4:5). The Gospel, however, is the final authority. "Perform your prayers and alms and all your acts as you have them described in the Gospel of our Lord" (15:4; cf. ch. 8; Matt. 6:1-15).

A more emphatic statement about almsgiving, based on the book of Tobit, occurs in 2 Clement 16:4: "Almsgiving is good as repentance is for sin; fasting is better than prayer, but almsgiving is better than both; love covers a multitude of sins, but prayer from a good conscience delivers from death. Blessed is everyone who is found full in these matters, for almsgiving lightens sin." Polycarp too speaks of almsgiving as delivering a man from death (10:2). Other writers similarly speak of works of charity. 1 Clement 8:4 quotes a

[24] A partial exception to this statement occurs in the correspondence of Pliny and Trajan; see pages 88-90.

passage from Isaiah 1:16-20 in which reference is made to aiding the orphan and the widow. Polycarp explicitly speaks of the presbyters' duty to care for the widow, the orphan, and the poor man (Phil. 6:1). Hermas speaks of someone named Grapte, who in the Roman church was accustomed to exhort the widows and orphans (Vis. 2, 4, 3) and says that the true servant of God will aid widows and look after orphans and those in need (Mand. 8, 10). The Christian businessman should purchase souls, not lands, and look after widows and orphans (Sim. 1, 8). Both deacons and bishops are responsible for these people (Sim. 9, 26, 2; 27, 2). Hermas gives practical counsel for caring for them. A Christian should fast, using nothing but bread and water for a day, and should keep an account of what he has saved, giving this sum to a widow or an orphan or someone in need (Sim. 5, 3, 7). A man who is rich does not have time for much intercession with the Lord; therefore he should give money to the poor man who has time to pray (Sim. 2, 5-7).

Another important function or aspect of almsgiving occurs in relation to hospitality, a virtue emphasized both in 1 Clement and in Hermas. Clement praises the hospitality of the Corinthian Church (1:2) and of Abraham (10:7), Lot (11:1), and Rahab (12:1); Hermas finds it characteristic of servants of God (Mand. 8, 10) and of bishops (Sim. 9, 27, 2).[25]

Its opposite, of course, is avarice or love of money, condemned in the Didache (3:5) and 2 Clement (6:4) and, especially, by Polycarp (Phil. 2:2, 4:1-3, 6:1). Hermas describes the situation of those whose riches darkened them a little; when their wealth was cut down but not wholly taken away, they were able to "live to God" (Sim. 9, 30, 5).

Among the Apostolic Fathers, Ignatius is the one who has the least to say about these matters. His relative silence can be explained in several ways. (1) He was not writing com-

[25] On this subject see H. Chadwick in *Texte und Untersuchungen* 79 (1961), 281-285.

plete treatises on faith and morals, and what he thought on
all subjects cannot be recovered from his letters. (2) He
may not have wished to encourage divisions between rich
and poor in communities already divided. (3) He may not
have wished to offer gratuitous advice on matters with which
he was not fully acquainted. Whatever the explanation of
his silence may be, we should remember that it is simply
relative. For in Smyrnaeans 6:2 he attacks the heterodox for
their lack of concern for love—and that, a love expressed
practically—as shown in care for the widow, the orphan,
the oppressed, the man either imprisoned or released, and
the hungry or thirsty. This statement, presumably based on
gospel teaching, clearly shows that Ignatius was concerned
with the practical aspects of community life. Again, in writing to Polycarp (4:1) he says that the widows are not to be
neglected and urges Polycarp to be their guardian "after the
Lord." Slaves are not to desire to be freed at the church's
expense (4:2), for the common fund is for the benefit of all.

This is to say that the teaching of the Apostolic Fathers on
the subject of money and almsgiving is fairly uniform. It
represents the normal approach already found in Hellenistic
Judaism and in the epistles of James, along with some ideas
apparently derived from the synoptic tradition. That we find
little from either Paul or John is not surprising; neither Paul
nor John has much to say on the subject.

As for *sexual ethics*, the same situation obtains. In the
Didache (2:2) we find an expansion of part of the Decalogue,
clearly related to comtemporary Jewish ideas. "Thou shalt
not kill, thou shalt not commit adultery (thou shalt not
corrupt children, thou shalt not commit fornication), thou
shalt not steal (thou shalt not use magic, thou shalt not use
philtres, thou shalt not kill a child by abortion nor put it to
death when born)." The pattern is clear: the Didachist con-
demns illicit sexual intercourse with women or with boys,
and he refuses to permit abortion or infanticide.[26] The same

[26] It is not clear whether or not contraception is treated as abortion.

ideas are repeated in Barnabas 19:4-5, and in allegorical exegesis of Leviticus in Barnabas 10:6-8. The statements reflect what we find in contemporary Jewish thought, especially in the Graeco-Roman world, and in the letters of Paul.

In the Shepherd of Hermas we find problems which have to do with marriage. For instance, the first Vision begins thus:

> He who brought me up sold me to a certain Rhoda at Rome. After many years I made her acquaintance again and began to love her as a sister. After some time I saw her bathing in the river Tiber, and I gave her my hand and helped her out of the river. When I saw her beauty I reflected in my heart and said, "I should be happy if I had a wife of such beauty and character." Thus was my only thought—no other.

Later, Rhoda—apparently deceased and therefore in heaven —appears to him and states firmly that "the desire of wickedness" did come up in his heart. Within little more than a year Hermas receives a revelation to the effect that henceforth his wife—the one he already has—is to be like a sister to him.

The psychological naïveté of this story is equaled only by that of another toward the end of the Similitudes (9, 11). In a vision, Hermas is in Arcadia, where he sees twelve virgins with whom he spends a night, sleeping with them at their request "as a brother and not as a husband"—though all of them kiss him before he lies down in their midst.

Such items can be explained as due to the author's intention to arouse his readers' interest—an intention shared with the writers of Hellenistic romances and for that matter of the Hellenistic (?) Jewish Testament of Reuben, which lingers over the account of a bath. They may also reflect concerns of his own.

The fourth of the Mandates is specifically concerned with marital problems. Desire for women other than one's own wife leads to sin, which can be prevented by remembering one's wife. But what if the wife herself is committing adultery

(she is assumed to be the Christian wife of a Christian)?
The Angel of Repentance answers this question in considerable detail. (1) As long as the husband is ignorant, he does
not sin. (2) If he knows of the sin, he implicitly participates
in it; he must separate from her, but he cannot remarry.
(3) If after separation the wife repents, she is to be received
back by her husband—but only once. This looks like a para-
phrase and expansion of the rules expressed by Paul in
1 Corinthians 7:10-16. Again, second marriages are permissible, but it is better for a widower or widow to remain
single—as in 1 Corinthians 7:40. The questions Hermas asks
may conceivably suggest the existence of certain difficulties
with his wife. More probably they show that the Church is
gradually developing a kind of canon law, or a precanonical
kind of law.[27]

Similarly, the remarks of Ignatius (Polyc. 5) about married
life and marriage suggest that he is developing what Paul
wrote in 1 Corinthians 7. Christian sisters are to love the
Lord and be content with their husbands "in flesh and spirit";
this resembles what Paul says about marital obligations in
1 Corinthians 7:3-4. The obligations, in Ignatius as in Paul,
are mutual, and husbands are to love their wives as the Lord
loved the Church (Pauline language from Eph. 5:25). Continence is permissible but must remain a private matter;
there is to be no boasting (cf. 1 Cor. 7:7). Finally, weddings
are to be under the direction of the bishop—probably because the bishop now occupies the place of the apostle, who,
as 1 Corinthians proves, exercised control over marriages.

The general picture which we can derive from the Apostolic Fathers confirms the statement of A. D. Simpson that
Christians were "quiet, busy people, living lives of mutual
help and trustfulness, and like the Epicureans refusing ambi-
tion, office-seeking and power."[28] At least two attitudes

[27] Cf. Acts 15:23-29; also E. Molland in *Studia Theologica* 9 (1955), 1-39.
[28] "The Good Citizen in the Second Century A.D.," *L'antiquité classique*
16 (1947), 78; her statement is based on the Apologists but applies to the
earlier period.

toward society, however, are reflected in their writings. On the one hand, Hermas insists that the slaves of God are living in a foreign country; their true city is far away from Rome or the empire and they make no use of Roman law (Sim. 1, 1-5). On the other, Clement gladly compares the Church to the Roman army and state (ch. 37) and insists that the Roman power is derived from God (61: 1-2). But even Clement does not express the enthusiasm for "the spirit of our time" which we find in Trajan's letter to Pliny (see page 90). And no Christian wrote anything like the oration of Aelius Aristides *To Rome,* a panegyric on the wonders of the city and of Roman rule.[29] In the early second century Christians were not at home in the world; they constituted a persecuted minority; their attitudes were like those of a sect, not those of a church. In the writings of their leaders, however—Clement, Ignatius, and Polycarp—there are already expressed the ideas which, following some apostolic precedents, were to reach fruition in the life and thought of the "great Church" which was to come.

[29] See S. Levin, *To Rome by Aelius Aristides* (Glencoe, Ill., 1950); J. H. Oliver, *The Ruling Power (Transactions of the American Philosophical Society,* XLIII, 4, [Philadelphia, 1953]).

BIBLIOGRAPHY

(*arranged chronologically*)

1. Texts and Translations

LIGHTFOOT, J. B., *The Apostolic Fathers*. 5 vols. London, 1885-90.
LIGHTFOOT, J. B., and HARMER, J. R. *The Apostolic Fathers*. London, 1891.
LAKE, K., *The Apostolic Fathers*. 2 vols. London and New York, 1912-13.
KLEIST, J., *The Apostolic Fathers*. Westminster, Md., 1946-48.
GOODSPEED, E. J., *The Apostolic Fathers*. New York, 1950.
RICHARDSON, C. C., *Early Christian Fathers*. New York, 1953.
BIHLMEYER, K., and SCHNEEMELCHER, W. *Die Apostolischen Väter*, vol. I. Tübingen, 1956.
WHITTAKER, M., *Der Hirt des Hermas*. Berlin, 1956.
JOLY, R., *Hermas: Le Pasteur*. Paris, 1958.

2. Dictionary and Word Index

ARNDT, W. F., GINGRICH, F. W., and BAUER, W., *A Greek-English Lexicon of the New Testament and Other Early Christian Literature*. Chicago, 1957.
GOODSPEED, E. J., *Index Patristicus*. Naperville, Ill., 1960.

3. Commentaries and Studies

a. Clement

KNOPF, R., *Die Lehre der zwölf Apostel. Die zwei Clemensbriefe*. Tübingen, 1920.
WINDISCH, H., "Das Christentum des zweiten Clemensbriefes," *Harnack-Ehrung*. Leipzig, 1921, 119-34.
SANDERS, L., *L'hellénisme de S. Clément de Rome et le paulinisme*. Louvain, 1943.
VAN UNNIK, W. C., "Is 1 Clement Purely Stoic?" *Vigiliae Christianae* 4 (1950), 181-189.
ZIEGLER, A. W., *Neue Studien zum ersten Klemensbrief*. Munich, 1958.

b. Ignatius

BAUER, W., *Die Briefe des Ignatius von Antiochia und der Polykarpbrief*. Tübingen, 1920.

SCHLIER, H., *Religionsgeschichtliche Untersuchungen zu den Ignatius-briefen*. Giessen 1928; with review by A. D. Nock in *Journal of Theological Studies* 31 (1929-30), 310-313.

RICHARDSON, C. C., *The Christianity of Ignatius of Antioch*. New York, 1935.

BARTSCH, H. W., *Gnostisches Gut und Gemeindetradition bei Ignatius von Antiochien*. Gütersloh, 1940.

PERLER, O., "Das vierte Makkabäerbuch, Ignatius von Antiochien, und die ältesten Märtyrerberichte," *Rivista di archeologia cristiana* 25 (1949), 47-72.

MAURER, C., *Ignatius von Antiochien und das Johannesevangelium*. Zurich, 1949.

BULTMANN, R., "Ignatius und Paulus," *Studia Paulina J. de Zwaan*. Haarlem, 1953, 37-51.

CORWIN, V., *St. Ignatius and Christianity in Antioch*. New Haven, 1960.

RIESENFELD, H., "Reflections on the Style and the Theology of St. Ignatius of Antioch," *Texte und Untersuchungen* 79 (1961), 312-322.

GRANT, R. M., "Hermeneutics and Tradition in Ignatius of Antioch," in E. Castelli, ed., *Ermeneutica e Tradizione* (Rome, 1963), 183-201.

c. Polycarp

See W. Bauer under "Ignatius" above.

HARRISON, P. N., *Polycarp's Two Epistles to the Philippians*. Cambridge, Eng., 1936.

VON CAMPENHAUSEN, H., Polykarp von Smyrna und die Pastoralbriefe," *Sitzungsberichte der Heidelberger Akademie der Wissenschaften* (Philos.-hist. Kl.), 1951, no. 2.

——, "Bearbeitungen und Interpolationen des Polykarpmartyriums," *ibid.*, 1957, no. 3.

d. The Didache

See R. Knopf under "Clement" above.

VOKES, F. E., *The Riddle of the Didache*. London, 1937.

DIBELIUS, M., "Die Mahl-Gebete der Didache," *Zeitschrift für die neutestamentliche Wissenschaft* 37 (1938), 32-41.

ADAM, A., "Erwägungen zur Herkunft der Didache," *Zeitschrift für Kirchengeschichte* 68 (1957), 1-47.

AUDET, J. P., *La Didaché: Instructions des apôtres*. Paris, 1958.

e. Barnabas

WINDISCH, H., *Der Barnabasbrief*. Tübingen, 1920.

MUILENBURG, J., *The Literary Relations of the Epistle of Barnabas and the Teaching of the Twelve Apostles*. Marburg, 1929.

PRIGENT, P., *Les testimonia dans le christianisme primitif: l'Epître de Barnabé I-XVI et ses sources*. Paris, 1961.

f. Hermas

DIBELIUS, M., *Der Hirt des Hermas*. Tübingen, 1923.

AUDET, J. P., "Affinités littéraires et doctrinales du Manuel de Discipline," *Revue biblique* 60 (1953), 41-82.

JOLY, R., "Judaisme, christianisme et hellénisme dans le Pasteur d'Hermas," *Revue des études anciennes* 5 (1953), 394-406.

BARBERET, F., "La formule zēn tōi theōi dans le Pasteur d'Hermas," *Recherches de science religieuse* 46 (1958), 379-407.

GIET, S., *Hermas et les Pasteurs*. Paris, 1963.

g. Papias

GUTWENGER, E., "Papias: eine chronologische Studie," *Zeitschrift für katholische Theologie* 69 (1947), 385-416.

MUNCK, J., "Presbyters and Disciples of the Lord in Papias," *Harvard Theological Review* 52 (1959), 223-243.

BEYSCHLAG, K., "Herkunft und Eigenart der Papiasfragmente," *Texte und Untersuchungen* 79 (1961), 268-280.

4. General Works

The New Testament in the Apostolic Fathers by a Committee of the Oxford Society of Historical Theology. Oxford, 1905.

WUSTMANN, G., *Die Heilsbedeutung Christi bei den Apostolischen Vätern*. Gütersloh, 1905.

KORN, H., *Die Nachwirkung der Christusmystik des Paulus in den Apostolischen Vätern*. Borna-Leipzig, 1928.

KLEVINGHAUS, J., *Die theologische Stellung der Apostolischen Väter zur alttestamentlichen Offenbarung*. Gütersloh, 1948.

TORRANCE, T. F., *The Doctrine of Grace in the Apostolic Fathers*. Edinburgh, 1948.

FLESSEMAN-VAN LEER, E., *Tradition and Scripture in the Early Church*. Assen, 1954.

KOESTER, H., *Synoptische Überlieferungen bei den Apostolischen Vätern, Texte und Untersuchungen* 65, Berlin, 1957.